HOW TO MAKE AN

AMERICAN HERO

AN AGE OF INNOCENCE

DANIEL EDWARDS MCCOY

God, Family, Country, and Corps

BLUEPRINT PRESS
INTERNATIONALE

ISBN
978-1-959365-22-8 (Paperback)
978-1-959365-23-5 (eBook)
978-1-959365-21-1 (Hardcover)

Dedication

This book is dedicated to my mother, Arlene McCoy, daughter, wife and mother of an American Hero.

ACKNOWLEDGMENTS

I'd like to thank my wife, Carla McCoy, for her expertise in helping me put this book together, obviously my better half.

CHAPTER

ONE

I feel that I must know more of my family history than it is possible for a young child to rationalize. Upon hearing this, my mother informed me that she had written her own memories down so her children could understand why we moved around so much. I have decided to rewrite my mothers' Memoirs into my book in order to respect my mother and to respect some of the heroes around whom I was raised. My Heroes have always been Christians. Here we go!

My mother was born in Missoula, Montana June 11, 1931. She said Grandpa Hay was in the middle of finals at the University of Montana when she entered the picture.

The family moved to Racine, Wisconsin when she was two years old. My mother remembers having a picture taken with her father, Grandfather and great Grandmother Hay. Grandma Hay was blind and 93 at the time and my mother was too young to understand her Grandmothers need to feel my mothers' face with her fingers and mother really objected to this invasion of her space. My mother also remembers having the measles while they were staying at her Grand parents' home and her father got in trouble for drawing pictures on the steamed windows to amuse his daughter, someone was going to have to clean that glass. My mother just wanted to go out and play in the yard with the sprinklers.

My mother' sister was born in Malta, Montana on March 13, 1935. Using that as a reference point, it must have been the beginning of the school year when they moved to Ukiah, Oregon in that same year. The family lived in the back of the country school. The school was partitioned off so that the living quarters were in the back section and the class room was

in the front. Her father had two high school students. Their parents each paid a hundred dollars a month so their children could have a high school education. Those people farmed and lived in a very isolated area of eastern Oregon. My mother was too young to go to school, but she figured that if she could hide beneath a chair and stay hidden until class started, she might get to stay in the class room. She thought she was well hidden, but when her dad saw her she still had to leave. I guess living in the school makes everyone family, because one of the students made my mom a pair of ski's out of barrel slats and she was devastated when one of the ski's broke.

For some reason it's significant to note, Marilyn always wore a bonnet as a child. I think it made it easier to find her in the tall grass.

My mother was hammering on a board on a sunny day when a wasp got under her arm and stung her. She let out a war hoop and her mom came running. That's what mothers do. She didn't understand the humor of the situation.

Her father was a Physicist/Scientist and the only TV and Radio repairman in the area. My mother was always curious as to what her dad was doing. One day she was watching him soldering a wire in a radio when a drop of solder fell on her foot resulting in another war hoop. She didn't understand the humor of that situation either.

The family moved to Stanfield, Oregon in 1936 until 1937. They lived in a nice house with hardwood floors. Grandpa was the school principal and also a teacher.

Mother had a little iron that was used for detailed or lace ironing. Small and powerful my mother left it on a leather seat of a dining room chair. It burned through the seat and was burning its' way into the hardwood floor when her father found it. She was very upset when her dad cut the end off of the cord so she couldn't heat it up again. This somehow resulted in the mud pies with frothy soap icing. They looked so good that she was able to talk Marilyn in her

beautiful bonnet to try some. My mother could not understand why her mother was not amused. My mother was fast approaching first-grade.

I find it curious that my mother remembers her childhood by things that offended her. She was caught chewing gum and the teacher made her sit up in front of her first-grade class, facing the classroom with the Black Jack gum on her nose. When she got home, her mom asked what was on her nose and my mom of course said I don't know, but the evidence of Black Jack gum must have stained her skin.

The kids had some freedom and one day they came to an old cabin. The old man that lived there had died and someone had thrown away some boxes of old spices. The kids had fun tasting, smelling and experiencing the flavors of all the spices.

My Grandpa was a ham radio operator and had a receiver that he had probably made himself. My mother slept in the bedroom on the other side of the wall. Grandpa would send Morse Code on the key and the noise would make it hard for her to sleep. One day she couldn't take

it anymore, so she took the largest tube out of the receiver and took it outside and buried it in a sand pile. In 1937 that tube cost 8 dollars and some people were working for fifty cents a day. When Grandpa found out what she had done, he spanked her. Her mother and sister were both crying so mother thought that they were afraid he might lose control and kill her. He never spanked her again, but she was never too sure that he wouldn't spank her again and she never messed with his ham radio equipment again.

Grandma and Grandpa Turpening lived close and not too far away, but it seemed like it took too long to get there. My mother was prone to car sickness. One time she was sitting between her mom and dad in a model A Ford and as a truck went by, a rock hit the windshield and the glass shattered all over them. Her dad said to sit still so they wouldn't get cut by the shards of glass. Luckily no one was hurt but it left a lasting impression. One reason we can be thankful for safety glass.

One of my mothers' fondest memories was Thanksgiving at Grandpa and Grandma Turpening, with aunts, uncles and cousins that she didn't see very often. Grandma Turpening was a large woman and an excellent cook. There was always a discussion as to whether the turkey was done. She doesn't remember ever having raw turkey. What she did remember was picking Goose berries for a Goose berry pie. It was alright until she tasted the pie and found out that to her it was awful. She hasn't eaten any since and doesn't know if she would try it again.

Another time after dinner, Grandpa Turpening and Jerry Southerland were sitting on the front porch smoking. My mother' parents didn't smoke so she had no access to cigarettes, so she took some walnut leaves and wrapped them in paper and she tried smoking in the outhouse. She thought she was going to choke to death and couldn't figure out how they could possibly enjoy smoking those cigarettes. My mother was at their home and remembers sleeping in the bathtub before it was installed

in the bathroom. Bathtubs were a luxury at that time, so it was exciting just to see one.

CHAPTER

THREE

One fond memory was of Grandpa Turpening on the roof of the two-story farm house, trying to get two kid goats off of the roof. He had been fixing something on the roof and had left the ladder against the house, and the two goats climbed the ladder and were playing on the roof. He managed to get the two goats and himself down off the roof safely, but it was both fun and scary watching the process.

Grandpa Turpening always had fun with my mother. He would offer a nickel in one hand and a dime in the other. She would take the nickel because it was bigger. He would laugh until she figured out it was a trick and learned to take the dime.

One Christmas Grandpa Turpening decided to get a Santa Claus suit and bring gifts in a large bag for all of the Grandchildren. My mother was about six at the time and she was the oldest Grandchild. In those days the only time you saw Santa Claus was in a book. Grandpa, with a big Ho-Ho-Ho, came in the front door with a Santa Suit on and big bag of presents, bedlam occurred. The children were scared half to death. One of them fell against the wood stove, burned, but not seriously, so Grandpa made a hasty retreat. That was enough of Santa that year.

My mother had a dog that got hit by a car. Her dad and Grandpa decided the injuries were too bad for the dog to survive and they were going to put it out of its misery and bury it. Grandpa told her to stay in the house. Instead she followed them to try to see what they were doing with her dog. Grandma Turpening caught her and took her to the woodshed and gave her a spanking. My mother was really insulted and wondered what business she had giving her a spanking.

My mother would sometimes sleep in Grandma Turpening big feather ticking/comforter. Grandma would put it over my mother and my mother felt like she was smothering. mother later realized that she was allergic to feathers after she got a non-allergic pillow years later. Once at Grandma's she was sleeping upstairs in a big bed and was awakened by an earthquake. Dishes were broken and it was really scary but no serious damage was done.

Grandma Turpening was an excellent seamstress. My mom could pick out a dress in the catalog and she would make my mom one just like it. It had smocking on the front and was very pretty. Grandma was a very no-nonsense type of person and Grandpa was a little too much fun loving. My mother felt he was a loving pest. My mother' mom felt that he didn't treat Grandma so good, but Grandma Turpening scolded Grandpa Turpening constantly. Mom believes they had a good relationship and Grandma gave as well as she got.

Grandpa Turpening had a lot of health problems when he got older and had cancer when

the love of his life died. Grandma Turpening went to a doctor because of a kidney infection and was given medication that she was allergic to. At that time mom believes they had nothing to counteract the allergic reaction and she died unexpectedly. Grandma Turpening died the day before my sister Patty was born September 23, 1952.

CHAPTER

★

FOUR

My mother started second grade in Eagle Point in 1938. Her father was one of three teachers of the Eagle Point faculty. Clarence Davies was the principle and teacher, Yetta Olsen teacher and Victor Hay taught science, mathematics etc. plus drove the school bus.

The Hay family attended church at the Eagle Point community church, which consisted of one room with a potbellied stove in the center of the room. There was an outhouse not too far away.

During Sunday school time there were two classes. Mrs. Esche was my mothers' Sunday school teacher for years. The other class was

for all the adults. The Esche Family owned a farm outside of Eagle Point; they were a very hard working people, had no children and filled their lives with and around missionaries and the Church.

The Eagle Point church was a mission of the Presbyterian Church and my mother accepted the Lord as her Savior at vacation bible school when she was 10 years old. At that time they had a Baptist minister named Keith Fields. He was not allowed to Baptize so they sent a Presbyter of the Presbyterian Church to baptize Bill Young and my mother. That means they were sprinkled not dunked. The preacher's wife was Sarah Fields; Sarah had a beautiful voice, played the piano and encouraged my mother to sing.

She was a lovely human being and had been raised in a Mennonite home. My mother thought it was hilarious, she advised all of the girls to get a sewing machine and round off all of their bras; it was a time of the sweater look and the bras were all pointy. My mother never saw a rounded off bra. I guess nobody took her advice.

One of my mothers' most memorable occasions happened when the congregation decided to end their relationship with the Presbyterian Church and choose to be independent. There were some harsh words in the meeting about not being grateful for the years the Presbyterian Church had kept the Church open. The church became the Eagle Point Community Church.

My mother' mom and dad bought a 1936 Ford sedan. It had been driven without oil and the engine had to be replaced but it was like new. My mother was with her dad when he brought it home and it was a very exciting time. That car was the one my mother learned to drive and was the vehicle my mom and dad used to go on their Honeymoon. During the war you couldn't buy a car of any kind and by the time my mother was in High School, everyone wanted that car because that's what all the cool cats drove if they could get one.

CHAPTER

FIVE

The family in Eagle Point lived in a trailer in the yard of the Young's house. Mr. Young was the Banker of the town. He liked the birds and trees around his house and he did not like mother cat. Moms' cat was a blue Persian and very docile and mom would dress him in doll clothes and make him lie in a doll carriage. My mom would get very upset if he didn't lie still and be nice. Once Mr. Young shot an owl that was after his birds and had it stuffed. My mother could not forget those big eyes as that owl sat on Mr. Young's desk. My mom visualized her cat being next. Later the family moved to a home on Kelso which later became

the parsonage of the Eagle Point Community church. The house had hard wood floors and my mom made her playhouse behind the piano. My mother remembers sticking her big toe in a broken socket that was on the floor. She received quite a jolt! That house was very comfortable, had a nice dining room, living room and a fire place.

On my mother' 18th birthday her mom said she could have a birthday party and asked her who she would like to invite to her party. My mother' request was Mr. and Mrs. Young and Dorothy, and Yetta Olsen. She had a very nice dinner with the people she wanted. They were all adults except for Dorothy and she was in high school.

Mother had a pet rat that her father had given to her. Everything went fine until the rat built a nest in her mother' linen drawer in the dining room and chewed holes in some of the linens. For some reason, that was the end of her pet. mother doesn't know what happened to the rat, but the rat was supposed to be a male.

The next move was into a rental, a small one-bedroom house owned by Mrs. Campbell. This was before my Uncle Fred was born. mother and her sister Marilyn started sleeping in Mrs. Campbell's house. mother remembers lying in bed watching her using a curling iron on her hair in the mornings. The curling iron was heated by an oil lamp and she would curl her hair around her face and then pull it back into a bun, which was quite stylish at the time. It actually looked more kinked than curled.

CHAPTER

SIX

Mother started taking piano lessons when she was seven and was able to practice on Mrs. Campbell's piano. She worked at the bank so mom was able to practice and experiment to her heart's content. Her lessons didn't last too long because her teacher would use a ruler to smack her on her knuckles when she made a mistake and she would hit her on her back if she didn't sit up straight. Her parents couldn't understand why she refused to go to her piano lessons. My mother continued to practice on her own and tried to figure it out on her own. She didn't take any more lessons until high school, then Mrs. Lang took some students

who already played the piano and agreed to give those lessons and helped them in what we wanted to do and needed help in. (Not very traditional piano lessons, at the time). When Mrs. Lang was carrying her baby, she turned her beginning pupils over to my mom to teach for a while. She, my mom, claims to have learned more from teaching the lessons than she learned from taking the lessons.

One of the most important things I have learned in my life is the concept of learning. You must be taught or Instructed by a teacher. You must be given time to contemplate the information. You teach the information to some interested party and the learning cycle continues. The reason Public schools are losing the fight is because they do not follow the rules of learning. Junior high students should teach Grade school. High school students should teach junior high, all under the supervision of a Teacher. The teacher must make sure that the students are not passing on misinformation.

My mother started playing the piano at church on Wednesday nights because the main

piano player only came on Sunday mornings. My mother couldn't play most songs all the way through so my mother has commented that she learned to play the piano because she didn't want to be embarrassed because she didn't know the whole song. Later after she got better, she played Sunday nights also. She says that the gifts that God gives us have to be cultivated and used and God will increase those gifts as God chooses if we chose to be led by the Lord. God must respect blood, sweat and tears.

CHAPTER

SEVEN

Mother remembers hearing Franklin Roosevelt on the radio saying that Japan had attacked Pearl Harbor and that we were at War. It was on a Sunday morning and he said "This day will go down in infamy".

When World War II was declared they started building Camp White right away. They first started building large tool sheds and then proceeded to the major building of barracks etc. Her father worked during the summer of 1942 as an electricians' helper which meant he dug a lot of ditches. She remembers him coming home quite upset because he was being harassed about being a sissy school teacher and she guesses that

he punched someone. He wasn't bothered after that, but it wasn't his nature to act like that and it really bothered him. He had been a light weight wrestling champion at the University of Montana and he had been in gymnastics so he could handle himself quite well. Mom doesn't remember him ever reacting like that again; it did affect his nerves during the War. Mom believes the children at school were hard to handle during those years and there was a lot of stress. Anger turns off children's ability to learn.

CHAPTER

★

EIGHT

My mother was chosen to be a cheer leader when she was a freshman in High School; she also participated in band and chorus classes. She accompanied the chorus some of the time and played the drums in the band. In her sophomore year she was class president. She was a cheer leader for two tears and at the beginning of her junior year she told Mr. Hale that she didn't want to be a cheer leader any longer. He objected but her reason was that the cheer leading costumes were too revealing. They wore sweaters and short skirts and most of the cheer leaders were well endowed. It was a time of the sweater girl influence. He told her that

they could change the cheer leading costumes if she objected, but she didn't want to be a cheer leader any more. She didn't object to the others being cheerleaders, she just didn't feel like the Lord was pleased with her being a cheerleader.

One of the many things she appreciated about her parents was that they let her make her own decisions when it was really important in her life. We believe that the only way a child can learn is to make decisions and suffer the consequence when young so they can learn to make good decisions when they get older. Life is one decision after another until the day that we die, and if we are not taught to make good decisions when we are young, the learning curve as an adult is miserable. In some things Grandpa and Grandma Hay made some of the more dangerous situations off limits. She wasn't allowed to be a vocalist in a local country western band. She was 15 and not allowed to go to the local dances. There was no objection to school dances or any school functions but the local dances at the Oasis and Brownsboro

tavern were pretty wild at that time. In other words, Off Limits!

Mother was in two plays in her junior year and was playing piano at the church after she had met my dad Herb. My father Herb was staying at Chris Holders house and had seen a class picture that mom was in. He told Chris that he wanted to marry that girl.

CHAPTER

NINE

Whathen my parents started going together my father had been a pitcher for the Brooklyn Dodgers farm team, they over pitched him and his shoulder was under a lot of strain. The reason my dad was in Oregon was to work in the woods in order to strengthen his arm. Uncle Ray was having trouble in California so they sent him to his big brother Herb.

Ray and Chris were in the same grade and were in some of my moms' classes at school. Later in life Ray and Chris got into a lot of trouble and seemed to bring out the worst in each other. Both were raised in Christian homes and though they had a rough time, they knew

that God was their only help in times of trouble. They had some time to think about it in prison.

The men that didn't go to War were criticized but her father was 36, with a family, he was a school teacher when the War started. He was invited to come to Washington D.C. to work on Radar but we lived in Oregon because of his wife's health. His wife was prone to lung problems that resulted in many bouts of pneumonia. The health problems associated with big cities then was worse than it is now. My Grandpa moved to Oregon because of the moderate temperature and he felt it would be easier on Grandma because she had weak and scarred lungs from chronic bronchitis from suffering pneumonia so many times before in her life. The Doctor had told him to enjoy her as much as possible because she was so weakened by chronic disease, the doctor didn't believe she would last long. Grandma Hay outlived Grandpa Hay into her 90's.

After Camp White was completed, Grandpa Hay bought two big tool sheds, sold one and dismantled the other one. There were no building materials for civilian use; everything was going to the war effort. With the recycled lumber he built the main part of his house near the small house we rented from Mrs. Campbell. Meanwhile he bought a piece of pasture land that was 7 acres, just outside the city limits. He moved the house he had built onto the pasture land. Grandpa paid cash for everything and very seldom took out a loan except for the loan on the property. So it was pay as you go. We had a large garden, chickens, ducks, and goats and raised beef calves for meat. They had a frozen food locker at the Butte Creek Mill and they froze vegetables and meat.

There were soldiers all over the place and mom rode to school with her dad most of the time on a bicycle. There were ration books for everyone in the family. Gas was rationed, as well as sugar, shoes and lots of other things. You could get Caro syrup for formula if you had a baby in the household. Mom imagined that it was easier if you lived in a farm community. It was encouraged for families to have victory gardens, even in the cities. It was possibly hard

on Grandma Hay, but mom wasn't aware of any hardship and their lives seemed quite secure even through the blackouts at night. All over the pacific coast there were blackouts at that time.

That meant that you had to have your windows covered so that no light would shine at night. That way there was no indication of a town or city from the air or the ocean.

During the War there was a shortage of young men in the area so my mom tried to help in the hay fields and also picked pears in the orchard. At the orchard we picked pears alongside German war prisoners. Of course they were well guarded and d we couldn't understand what they said, which in hind sight, was probably a good thing. They would have arts and crafts shows at Camp White showing what some of the German war prisoners had done while they were imprisoned. Some of the projects were really very good.

When my mother was 13 a soldier asked my mom to marry him. She hadn't even gone with him or even kissed him. He was a Christian and went to our church, but she wasn't interested in marrying anyone at that time. I'm sure the

folks were shocked but mom didn't look like she was 13 either. The soldiers trained at Camp White married a lot of local girls before they had to leave for the front. Mom thought they were quite desperate to have something to come home to and many of them didn't come back.

CHAPTER

TEN

My Grandfather was mayor of Eagle Point, Oregon during the Second World War; at least my mom knows he was Mayor when she was in the seventh grade.

In 1947 mom's dad took them on a vacation for the summer and they traveled through Montana. He showed them where the old homestead was located. He said he didn't know how his parents survived homesteading in Montana. This was near Broadview, Montana and was where both her mom and dad graduated from high school. They also stayed a week in Yellowstone Park. At that time you could stay and camp inside the park. We had a small trailer called a Teardrop.

Grandma, Grandpa and Aunt Ellen slept in the Teardrop. Aunt Marilyn mom and Uncle Fred slept in the car.

They were able to see a concert pianist at the lodge in Yellowstone Park. After the applause you could hear Uncle Fred say "I can hit it harder!" I have no idea what he meant by that. They visited Uncle Clarence and Aunt Hazel in Livingston, Montana which was just outside of Yellowstone. My mom got a Montana driver's license while she was there. She used the Turpening address and didn't have to take a written test or a driver's test to get her license so she could help with the driving. When she got back to Eagle Point she was the only fifteen year old with a drivers' license. My mother and Aunt Marilyn did a lot of singing on that trip for amusement.

They went to Racine, Wisconsin where her dad's folks lived; also his two sisters and a brother with their respective families lived also. Moms' Grandpa was a coin collector and would spend the evenings going through bags of coins from the bank. He would replace any coins that

he found and wanted to keep and take the bags back to the bank in the morning. They went to the Baptist church on Sunday with Grandma.

We went to Chicago, Illinois and visited a market place where there were people of all nationalities selling things in the market place in the streets. Mom had never seen so many different kinds of people and it was fascinating. She also got to ride on a subway. Everything was moving too fast for a country girl. They visited the lake where Uncle Wally and Aunt Vi had a summer home. They had a lot of fun boating on the lake and playing with the cousins.

CHAPTER

ELEVEN

When mother was in the seventh grade she had a real crush on a young man, Tommie Ireland. He was in the eighth grade, so he decided to fail the eighth grade so he could spend more time with my mother, who was a grade behind him. His family didn't go to church and he didn't have much interest in things like that. She told Tommie later that they shouldn't go together if he didn't have any desire to go to church or have any interest in the Lord. Shortly after that, Tommie and a girl eloped and got married in Klamath Falls, Oregon. Their parents found out and brought them back to Eagle Point, Oregon and had their marriage

annulled. mother doesn't believe that they were really in love. She believes that Tommie was too young for that kind of decision. She believes that they were secretly relieved when their parents stepped in and put a stop to the situation. Mom believes the couple did it to spite her. From that time on when Tommie would try to date or try to be with mom, she wouldn't because he had been married. For my mom it was quite a temptation because she really did like him. I thank God for my mothers' discretion at that time. Tommie quit school and mom didn't see him much after that.

When mom was 15 and after they had returned from their trip to Racine, Wisconsin, Tommie was killed in an accident when they were moving a house on a job he had. He was on the roof and was electrocuted. Years later when my mom and dad were in Brookings, Oregon on the coast, Herb McCoy (Dad) was singing and speaking at a Full Gospel Business Men's Meeting. Tommie's sister Rosie and her mother came to the meeting and Rosie showed my mother a couple of pictures of her that they

had found in Tommie's wallet after he had been killed 30 years previous.

CHAPTER

TWELVE

When mom was 16 she met my dad, Herb McCoy. He came to church with Beth and Claude Turner, who were the young peoples' leaders. They asked him to sing and mom was playing the piano. He sang When They Ring the Golden Bells. Her dad said it wasn't Golden Bells, it was Wedding Bells. For mom it was love at first sight. She had met the man that God had planned for her life. She said that she could have gone in another direction except the Lord protected her and she knew that she could not be unequally yoked together with an unbeliever. Dad and mom were married August 29, 1948, at the Eagle Point Community church

by Reverend Floyd Pollock. Eileen Pollock was my moms' maid of honor and Claude Turner was my dad's best man. Mom had just finished her junior year of High School so her Parents asked that my mom finish high school so my mom dropped band, chorus and all the classes that were not required Married and going to school was a difficult chore. They were living in a cabin by the Rogue River in Shady Cove, Oregon and mom had to ride in a school bus for the first time in her life.

At that time the other parents didn't really appreciate their kids going to school with married students, even though many of those parents had dropped out of school because they were pregnant. My Grandfather took a lot of criticism for letting his daughter get married at seventeen because he was an educator. I guess my Grandfather didn't believe in keeping his children as pets. I guess my mother had a mind of her own.

My father Herb McCoy was a Christian, he was 22 years old and he had a beautiful singing voice and had a very persuasive personality.

Moms' parents loved him too. Grandpa thought my father was the best looking man he had ever seen. He also believed that my father would never be satisfied with anything in his life. My mother often thought of my Grandfathers' statement and believed her dad was very perceptive. That may be the reason they were never critical of the many places we lived and the things we went through.

My father, Herb McCoy felt that life was an adventure and he wanted to do something different and move to somewhere different. My father loved people in general. He had no trouble making friends and was always interested in their food and culture. He was always a testimony for the Lord Jesus Christ. My mother never doubted that he loved her or the children. He was always faithful and dependable.

My mother had never met any of my fathers' relatives except for Uncle Ray. One day there was a knock on the door and there stood a man who said he was my father's father. He had hitch hiked from California to see Herb and the girl he had married. Grandpa Bob and Grandma

Louise McCoy later moved to Oregon and lived and worked in a pear orchard. It was hard work and the living quarters were not ideal but Grandpa and Grandma McCoy loved their children and seemed to survive on a good sense of humor and a wonderful work ethic.

In the middle of my mother' senior year, my father, Herb decided to go to Bible School in Seattle, Washington at Simpson Bible Institute. My mother had enough credits to graduate but had to finish two books that were requirements. Mr. Hale had her outline those two books and she graduated with her class in 1949 even though she was in Seattle at the time.

CHAPTER

THIRTEEN

In January 1949 my parents Herb and Arlene McCoy went with Pat and Annie Patzke to Seattle so my dad could go to Simpson Bible Institute. Mom and dad hadn't planned ahead so it took a little time for the G.I. Bill to take effect. They stayed in an apartment with Pat and Annie Patzke until my parents could afford an apartment of their own. One day my father left the keys in Pats' car and that night the car was stolen. This not only caused embarrassment and inconvenience, it was one of the trials that had to be endured when you are careless and too trusting and trying to adjust to the crime of big cities. The theft of the car left both families

without transportation so we all learned to use public transportation/bus.

Their first apartment was near campus and it was just a bedroom and bath. Mom and dad ate their meals on campus while mom worked as a cooks' assistant to pay for their meals.

In the summer mom and dad moved into a downtown church called Bethel Temple into a small apartment so my dad, Herb could sing over on a radio broadcast every morning at 7:00 AM; my mom would accompany him on the pipe organ. They had a ten minute broadcast every morning. It seemed like Grand Central Station because the apartment was so handy to the church. My mother was pregnant at the time and had a lot of morning sickness. She said it took a lot of crackers and hard candy for her to get through those radio broadcasts and it was miserable for her. She now thinks it was the bus fumes that bothered her so much because after they moved from down town she wasn't bothered so much.

They moved into an apartment where they shared a kitchen and bathroom but had three

rooms to themselves. The house belonged to a retired nurse. She had a dog that she cooked for. He was a Cocker Spaniel and would beg for raw carrots.

That fall Grandpa and Grandma Hay moved to Seattle. Her dad, Victor Hay had taken two years off from teaching at Eagle Point, Oregon so he could go to bible school. A friend Warren Christianson was already in school. Marion and Chuck Sturgil moved to Seattle at the same time as mom' folks and were living with mom's parents in the Ballard section.

Everyone came to the same conclusion that it would be better for everyone involved if mom and dad would move in with moms' parents, and Chuck and Marion would move into my parent's apartment. Mom, Arlene believes that the Sturgils had two boys at the time. It was very difficult to find a place to live comfortably and reasonably, everyone was pinching pennies to survive.

Mom's parents had bought property with two houses on the lot. One of the houses was rented and later after the original tenants left

the Browns rented that house. They lived there a couple of years. Mom's dad had a job and the students were sneaking out at the Bon Marche doing radio repairs and learning to be a TV technician.

Her dad was going to Bible School as well and was very busy. My father, Herb was going to Bible School and was singing in the downtown churches. Simpson was a closed campus and the students were sneaking out to go see the Pentecostal revivals in the downtown churches. The churches were Pentecostal and strictly off limits.

Later my parents went to church at the Seattle Revival Center. Ralph Sanders was the Pastor and they were in the middle of a revival at the church. The place was packed night after night with many people at the altar seeking the Lord. The evening services had a natural stopping point because there was always a live radio broadcast every night at 10:00. My father sang solos many nights. Marilyn and Darlene sang duets and my mother occasionally sang with them as a trio. Moms' dad, Victor played

the violin in the church orchestra a lot of times during church services.

FOURTEEN

My parents were staying at Grandma and Grandpa's house when I was born at the Swedish Hospital in Seattle on February, 9, 1950. She says I looked like a little Papoose. She believes that I got a lot of the Native American Indian genetics from my dad except I had blue eyes. She says that I would batt my eyes every time someone would mention my beautiful eyes because they were striking with my long dark eyelashes. I guess that I have the genetics of my Grandmother on my dad's side of the Lakota Siox, Choctaw, Chickasaw and Cherokee Nations, to thank for my dark hair and thick eyelashes.

It was hard for my father to be in bible school because there was a revival going on at the school too. There were several people speaking in tongues in the dorms and when brought to the attention of the President of the school he decided to put an end to the practice. His quote was "I know that speaking in tongues is in the bible but we don't want it here". My father felt that he couldn't stay in a place that rejected something that was so important in his life. Previously they had said that they believed in being filled with the Holy Spirit and that you could choose to speak in tongues or not. A.B. Simpson, who founded the Christian Missionary Alliance church, was definitely a believer in the power of God and the miracles that follow those who believe. My father was ordained into the ministry at the Seattle Revival Center by Ralph Sanders.

My parents decided to move back to Oregon and my father got a job in the woods. We were living in a log cabin in Prospect Oregon. My mother had to learn to chop wood and cook on a wood stove. She will never forget the

frustration of trying to make an angel food cake at high altitude in a wood cook stove… what a disaster!!! We were only a short time there because my father was in the Naval Reserve. He was called back to active duty. The Navy was short on radio operators and the Korean War was in full swing. My parents decided that the best place for mother and me was in Seattle with her and her folks. So we packed up and drove to Seattle and my father left for Korea. My mother didn't know at the time, she was pregnant with my sister Linda Carol McCoy.

CHAPTER

★

FIFTEEN

Linda Carol McCoy was born March 21, 1951 in an Army Hospital in Seattle, Washington. The Army nurses didn't think that they should pamper patients. A nurse came in with some sheets and linen and asked if my mother wanted to make her bed. She, the nurse said she would make the bed today, but my mother would be expected to make it herself the next day. My baby sister Linda had just been born at 4:00 AM and my mom said she didn't feel like making it today, so the nurse made the bed. They had told her to lay flat for 12 hours because of the spinal injection they had given her for pain. The nurse decided to ignore the doctor's orders and

decided to roll up my mom's bed so my mother could eat breakfast. My mother told the nurse that she was supposed to lie flat for 12 hours, and mother had some very severe headaches as a result of the incompetence of that nurse. My father was outside of Korea on a salvage ship when Linda was born so the Navy sent him a pink telegram. I suppose if the baby had been a boy it would have been a blue telegram.

Two months after my sister Linda was born, my Grandfather Bob McCoy died; the story is that my Grandfather was found breathing through a hole in a sawdust bin. He prayed to his father the Creator to preserve him so he could get his affairs in order. He was rescued. He got his affairs in order and in two weeks he died.

The doctors claimed that when my Grandfather who had been a professional boxer, he had a burst appendix that resulted in an internal infection that weakened his body as one of the contributing factors in his death.

I had the measles so I was left in Seattle with my Grandma Hay while my mom and sister

Linda went to Medford, Oregon. They put off the funeral for ten days so my father could get there in time for the internment. My mother said that the first time my sister Linda saw our father she just smiled and smiled.

The McCoy family was all there for their dads' funeral, the first and possibly the only time they were all together. There were eleven children in the family and six were still at home when Grandpa Bob McCoy died. Grandma Louise McCoy's maiden name was Morgan. She took great pride in her own family tree; she said she followed the McCoy's back to a guy hung for stealing a horse.

She then traced her family back to Colonel John Johns of the continental Army. He was married to one of the daughters of the Salem Tobacco farm. That of course meant we were related to the Daniel Morgan that rescued the Revolutionary Army because he brought the weapons technology of the mountain men of Kentucky along with the Mountain men that assisted the colonies to push the British off the continent.

Guns are at the very core of being an American, alongside the production of Alcohol and the production of Marijuana/Hemp. It required five acres of hemp in order to manufacture the needs of a single naval vessel. I think it is time for America to quit charging my Scottish Ancestors the tax for the war. It is time to quit criminalizing their way of life through life killing taxation. I believe the ATF is a redundant arm of the FBI and needs to be retired.

My Grandma, Louise Morgan McCoy was a woman of God and depended upon the creator to carry her through the rough times. Can you spell Holy Roller?

My mom and dad went back to Seattle and then my dad had to return to San Diego, California. The Navy decided to return my dad to inactive reserve but it would take a couple of months.

My mother took myself and Linda on a greyhound bus from Seattle, Washington to San Diego, California, that was quite a trip with two young babies. My mother was nursing Linda and I was an active 16 month old toddler.

The disposable diapers were a disaster at that time (1951) when they got wet they seemed to disintegrate. At that time the back of the bus was all the way across the back off the bus and if the bus was not too crowded, my sister and I could lie down and sleep for a while. Linda was a very good baby and I was a handful, hard to keep settled down.

We stayed in a roach coach motel until my parents could afford a small trailer to live in until my father got released from the Navy. The thing my mother remembers most from that time, was an ice cream truck that would drive through the park and wake me up from my nap. My parents bought a car and drove back to Seattle when my father was released from the Navy.

CHAPTER

SIXTEEN

Our family went to Wenatchee, Washington to sing and help in a church there with Rev. Richard Vaughan, his wife and family. There was a lot of dissention in the church and Reverend Vaughan accepted the Pastorate of an independent church in Granite City, Illinois. He asked my family if we would come along, so of course we packed up all of our belongings and drove to Granite City Illinois.

My parents were so low on funds that when they had a flat tire on the trailer they had to send for 25 bucks from Grandma and Grandpa Hay for another tire.

We rented an upstairs apartment and my father got a job in a steel mill and he was minister of music at the church. My father wasn't paid for the time he spent for the church or the time he travelled with Pastor Vaughan.

My mother was miserable in that apartment because the people had only rented the space because the husband was ill and they had to somehow replace his wages. They didn't want any visitors past 9 PM. The difficulty of trying to keep her kids quiet was making my mom quite stressed out. It seemed to keep us kids on edge and crying all the time.

The stress of that apartment my father took a job in a fish market outside of town because there was a house provided with the job. They sold fresh fish that they kept in fish tanks. People would pick the one they wanted and they would butcher the fish while the customer waited. My dad would drive to St. Louis, Missouri and bring back tanks of live fish; it was a very busy fish market. We finally had a nice yard and plenty of room.

My father bought a Honkey Tonk piano for 25 dollars he had found in St. Louis at a bar. Mom said it was a good sounding but hard to look at with all the drink circles all over it.

We lived there in E. St. Louis when my sister Patricia Ann was born. My mother carried her past her due date about three weeks and she weighed 9lb. 13oz.

My mom and dad were at all the services at the church. My mom played the piano and my father led the music and sang solo's.

The pastors' wife told my mother she would help mom after she got out of the hospital but my mom came home to dirty dishes in the sink and a dirty house. My mother was so mad she just washed the dishes, mopped the floor and went to bed. I guess she showed her.

Patty was a wonderful baby; she only woke us up for feeding the first night, and slept through the night most of the time.

In the pastors' wife's favor, she had visiting pastors at her house. Being the perfect hostess is difficult and she simply bit off more than she could chew. Patty had come three weeks late

and had screwed up everyone's schedule. The pastor's wife did take care of my sister and me in the daytime for my dad when dad was working and mom was in the hospital.

The Christians were expecting everyone else to give of themselves with nothing in return, they weren't concerned about others. They didn't realize that God is the original Jew and a workman is worthy of his hire. They didn't seem to realize that the tithe of 10% of their congregations' time cannot be taken for granted. In spite of the narcissism and self-serving ignorance of the Church Board of Directors, the Lord was working and there were some close friends who became committed Christians. Bert Boone, wife of Harvey Boone, was already a Christian, but Harvey was real bitter about the church. My dad was able to convince him that you don't allow disobedient Christians stop you from service to the Lord. The important thing is to love the Lord thy God and follow him. I would add love learning and choose to goodness all of your days.

Later one of Harvey Boone's children became an Assembly of God Pastor. Harvey died of a heart attack at the early age of 55 and his family is serving the Lord.

When we were in Bonners Ferry, Idaho, my dad Herb flew to Granite City, Illinois to sing at Harvey's funeral. Bert came to visit mom after dad died, to tell mom how much our influence had been on her family and how much she appreciated it.

CHAPTER

SEVENTEEN

I was born in Seattle Washington, February the 9th in the year, 1950, to my parents' Herbert Allen McCoy and Eva Arlene McCoy, at the Sand Creek Naval Hospital. My father was studying at a Seminary School.

My father had been called back to the Navy from his Seminary School in Seattle to continue his service to the Navy; he was in an in-active reserve status from World War II. When my father reported for duty, the sailors found out that he had been in Seminary School to become a Minister. They decided to find out if they could get him drunk and when they did he preached to them for four hours straight, and

from that day on, no one was allowed to give Herb McCoy more than one drink.

My father was a man who did not trust the opinions of other men. If he did not receive inspiration from his own readings, "God is no respecter of persons" therefore, if my father did not understand the meaning of the written word as explained by other men, his malarkey detector went off. The Bible interprets itself in verse; context or it has been explained before in scripture. The only thing that we have to take on Faith is to believe that Jesus Christ is the son of God and that God lifted his son, Jesus Christ, from the grave after Jesus Christ had lain dead in his tomb for three days.

CHAPTER

EIGHTEEN

My childhood memories of my life before we moved to Oklahoma are very vague. I remember a baseball park and excited people. My father was always the center of attention because he was the pitcher and he could hit. This was true all of my life, even though his one year with the Brooklyn Dodgers blew out his right shoulder, ending his professional sports career. This always confused me, because I saw him pass a football and punt a football, end post to end post.

When he went to a golf ball driving range, they would take away his driver and made him use a five iron, because he could consistently

drive a Golf ball three hundred yards with a driver. I believe he always preferred preaching the Gospel and singing over sports.

He took great enjoyment from beating his younger brother, the professional Golf Pro in Oklahoma, my father was a freak of Nature when it came to Sports, and he was also the finest vocalist I have ever known.

I had a stigmatism in my right eye, and that eye being my dominate eye, things were not exactly where I thought them to be. I hit a lot of batters. I diligently threw the ball where I saw it. I should have been taught Kentucky Windage. I was taught Kentucky Windage when it came to shooting, but somehow I could not relate it to my eyesight. If a rifle has fixed sights, you must know how far off the sights are and make adjustments accordingly. You must also allow for wind and movement.

My early childhood thoughts were of being trapped in the back of a nineteen forty-nine Ford Coupe with my sisters and the rear windows would not roll down. My father seemed to be delighted when he would pass gas and would

wait to roll down the front window until we would make gagging and puking noises, waiting until we begged him to roll down the window.

My father wanted us to eat beans with onions and corn bread every Friday night. This was to remind us of the depression when that was all his family could afford to eat. I don't buy that for a second. My Grandfather, Robert McCoy, was a State Representative for the State of Oklahoma and they owned a Bakery in Oklahoma City. My family believes that they so miss-managed my Grandmother certified Native American trust land, that a bank in Washington D.C. took over my families land and still holds it in trust. It's not supposed to be possible to confiscate certified Native American Trust Land; they say the bank was owned by the Brother of the President of the United States at the time. Do you think they pulled off a fast one?

CHAPTER

NINETEEN

My father had a mean sense of humor when it came to his children going on dates. Beans, raw onions and corn bread are the perfect ingredients for discomfort. It meant a miserable gas filled Friday and Saturday night for the rest of us. Later on it limited the quality of dating as well. I wonder if that is why they call it the family pew.

I was two or three when we moved into a log cabin on the tree line of Mount Pit in the state of Oregon. It was possibly the most beautiful place I had seen at that point of my life. The cabin was a one room affair with blanket dividers for privacy. We had a seep spring out the back door

for water and a wood cook stove for heat and cooking. We used kerosene lamps for light. My parent's bed was a partial loft and their walls were Quilts hung from the ceiling.

My sisters and I would go across the meadows full of wild flowers to the pine trees to search for pine sap on the trees for the cook stove. Pine sap made it easy to start the fire in the cook stove.

My sisters', running through the wild flowers, was like a magic picture, their blonde hair looking like a halo flowing through the multi-colored flowers. Our hound dog was bounding along looking like he was dancing, ready to protect us from the wild things, until one day he chanced upon a porcupine.

We woke up one morning to a great wailing and moaning. We rushed outside to see our great protector with a mouth and nose full of quills. We tried to pull them out, but it seemed to hurt him more. When my father came home, we had to hold him while my father took his wire cutters and cut off the end of the quills, which promptly released the vacuum and the quills came out easily. Porcupine quills seem

to create a vacuum when they enter flesh and the vacuum must be removed before pulling them out or they take a lot of flesh with them. I remember it happened again, but the second time was not as traumatic as the first.

Somehow I seem to have gone through Oregon, Indiana and Illinois without any traumatic memories. I know my father worked as a picture Framer and fish butcher.

CHAPTER

TWENTY

We moved to Oklahoma to a farm in Medford. We inherited about twenty barn cats that our Weiner dog enjoyed hunting. We liked to run around on the outbuildings until my sister fell on the chicken pen and got her leg impaled on a heavy wire. My father had to lift her off the wire, which for me was quite traumatic to endure.

Oklahoma was where we took part in wheat harvest and found out that if you chewed raw wheat it turned into chewing gum. Who would have thought that our most popular grain had to be cooked to eat it?

The wheat flowed in the wind like the waves on the ocean. The wheat fields were beautiful. When the wind blew, the wheat looked kind of like the ocean of motion that went up and down hills like the froth on a large wave.

The most enjoyable times I remember occurred on occasional Fridays, I call it the Oklahoma Friday Night. The day would start with my father and me going to the crawfish pond with a ten foot seine net. We would drag the bottom of the pond and fill buckets with crawfish. The pond was in a region of red dirt. Willow trees seemed to be the predominant foliage. There were Lilly pads and brush in some places. I remember we could fish for sunfish there at the pond.

The worship team and church members would pack up provisions for fried potatoes and hush puppies and all of us would head out to a sand bar on the river. We had an old row boat and trotlines that we strung across the river. All of the females, young and old started cooking enormous iron skillets of bacon, onion and fried potatoes. They made cornmeal batter for the

fish and hushpuppies. We always caught catfish, soft shell turtles and perch. There were campfire songs and gospel songs to the tune of guitars. The fellowship was wonderful.

We checked the trot lines every couple of hours. The lines were strong enough to pull the rowboat so the lines went across the boat. That was fun because you never knew what was on the lines. Snakes and eels, soft shelled turtles, alligator snapping turtles, big and small catfish, basically everything eats crawfish.

The soft shelled turtles seemed to all have long necks. You have to know how to handle soft shelled turtles or they will reach around and bite you. Luckily, if you catch a snake the snake usually have a hook in their mouth. If you don't know how to handle snakes, I highly recommend you cut off their head before you take them off the line.

A rowboat gets very crowded when a Cotton Mouth Water Moccasin drops off the line into the boat. The commotion is almost as much fun when an alligator snapper gets loose in the boat. Catfish are just about as dangerous in a

boat because of their fins, and you can receive an extremely painful wound from a catfish.

CHAPTER

TWENTY-ONE

My family lived in the middle of a wheat field when I experienced my first Tornado. It seemed that we lived in an ocean of flowing green. The wheat flowed like water as the wheat grass responded to the wind pressure. The rain was so heavy that the clouds blocked out the sun. The cloud looked like a wall of fury as it advanced across the flowing plains. As it advanced upon our house the first to arrive was the rain. It rained so hard that we couldn't see. It was so dark it seemed like night. The rain was flowing in huge torrents. Suddenly it got deathly quiet, and when the rain suddenly stopped my father commanded us all into the Tornado shelter. The television warned us of the

tornado in our region as we hurried to get into the storm shelter. As we were running to the shelter which was in the basement, the television station went off the air. I looked back at the picture window and I saw the eye of the tornado peering through the glass.

For many years I believed that I saw the actual eye of the storm until I realized it was the CBS logo reflecting from the television onto the picture window. Believe half of what you see and very little of what you hear. Always check your facts. Memorization in our schools has led many people astray. Do the work to check the foundation of what you memorize. It's easy to be misled when you memorize facts without researching the facts. This tornado resulted in our move to Mississippi.

CHAPTER

TWENTY-TWO

I love Mississippi because it is where I grew up. We went fishing and hunting all the time to survive the poverty, but I didn't know we were poor. My father worked on an off shore drilling rig. One day he was loading drill pipe by hand when the crane operator knocked him into the basket. My father suffered a blood clot in his leg and he lost his job. My mother had a miscarriage and I had to learn to cook breakfast for my sisters. I think I liked it and I still like to cook.

When my father was hurt on the offshore drilling barge, we lived for two years on unemployment insurance at $53 a week. That

was possible because of the house that we were given and all of the fishing, crabbing and hunting we did for recreation and food. There was a bread store where we got day old bread by the feed bag. We could get shrimp off the boats for three dollars a pound. In special times we bought half a gunny sack of oysters for two dollars. We would go crabbing, boil crabs and put newspaper all over the table and eat all the crab we could hold. Mom let us bring home a bag of shells from the beach and in the middle of the night they were crawling around the kitchen. There were hermit crabs in the shells. We kids had great time hunting around the house for the hermit crabs.

My mother did a lot of sewing for us children and other people. My Aunt Connie Curry would send boxes of Cousin Cindy's clothes that were in excellent condition and mother would alter them for my sisters. Connie would complain because her mother-in-law would buy all of Cindy's clothes and so consequently Cindy had more clothes than she could possibly wear. We

were really thankful for her consideration and our family thanked the Lord for Aunt Connie.

My mother had an agreement to sew for one of her friends in exchange for patterns and material for herself comparable to what my mother made for her. I guess those seven years of 4-H learning to sew came in mighty handy when things got tough. I do believe that we are doing our young girls a disservice when they are not taught home economics.

Sister Beale gave my mother money for a winter coat and mom bought a sewing machine instead. Buy a coat and be warm for a year, buy a sewing machine and everyone can be warm forever. Sister Beale was pastor of a large church in Detroit, Michigan, and was a frequent guest speaker at the Revival Center in Gulfport, Mississippi. Her ministry had started years ago when she would go door to door with her children bundled up in the wagon and she would minister to people. She said times were so rough that she couldn't afford underwear but she knew how to minister to people on their own level. Her church grew until it had thousands

of members and every year they bought her a new Cadillac. She was always aware and very sensitive of other peoples' needs. Later when she retired, her son James Beale became pastor of Bethesda Missionary Temple. The Thompson chain reference that my father ministered with for years was given to him by a black lady in sister Beal's church when he was singing there.

CHAPTE

TWENTY-THREE

In the second grade we played football in full uniform, I loved that too even though I was the smallest kid in school. I was so small that I learned to tackle from the ground. I called it a shoestring tackle. I may not have been big, but I had a strong grip. I often found myself buried in bodies as I reached up to trip a runner. My wrestling opponents were all bigger than me. It seemed everyone was bigger than me.

We moved to the airport at that time and we lived in an abandoned restaurant. It also had a baseball field behind the house. I was so small that we couldn't find a real baseball mitt to fit my hand. I played second base with a little

red rawhide baby glove that lacked the proper padding in the thumb. I now have a double jointed left thumb because of baseballs hitting the end of my thumb. I remember having dreams that I was running from the baseball field to go to the bathroom at home as I woke up wetting the bed. The dream seemed so real.

There was always fighting, school, fighting and baseball. I was wrestling with Ralph. Ralph stood between me and baseball. We were fighting in some ones front lawn. Ralph was five foot seven and weighed one hundred and twenty pounds. I was five feet tall and ninety five pounds. We really weren't hurting each other or should I say, I wasn't hurting him. Two teenage girls ran out to break up the fight. That singular incident was the most fun I ever had as a result of a fight. The girls were holding us apart as they tried to control our rage. I somehow forgot all about the fight. They were soft in all the right places and they smelled really nice, so it was easy to forget the fight. In grade school your opponents are somehow your friends. Ralph was big enough to pass for an adult and was killed

driving a car when he was twelve. I actually was distraught when he died.

I and my father always went hunting or fishing whenever we could to supplement our food supply. I thought it was for fun, I knew it was necessary for my family. My father was paid three hundred and fifty dollars a month as a deputy sheriff, but he had five kids. We received commodities from the United States Department of Agriculture. The food we received was always of a quality we could not afford to buy.

The poorest people in America get the best food we produce in America. One of my favorite meals was chicken and dumplings made from canned chicken. We would take the bones out of the chicken. We reserved the sauce from the can. We mixed in a can of mixed vegetables, usually called succotash and then my mother would make dumplings to put on top. We called it chicken and dumplings. I also liked it if we cut dinner flour tortillas into one inch strips and added a cup of chicken broth to the mixture, instead of the biscuits.

My father would make Spanish rice with canned ham. He would make a sauce of brown sugar, onions, mustard and cayenne pepper. He would dice the spam into cubes and brown them before he put the spam chunks in the sauce. He would cook two cups of rice and when the rice was done he would mix the sauce and rice together. He called the concoction Spanish rice. I believe that if you take out the sugar and Spam, and replace it with a pound of hamburger, chopped peppers and celery, you can have dirty rice.

CHAPTER

TWENTY-FOUR

I remember one time we were hunting squirrels and my father had given me a bolt action, twenty gage shotgun, with which I was supposed to hunt rabbits. He was in the woods and I was in a meadow to hunt rabbits. I saw an animal bounding through the grass that was black with white spots. I was not aware as to what it was. My father thought it might be a domestic rabbit gone wild so he told me to shoot it and throw it in the back of the pickup truck. I shot it and threw it in the back of the pickup and when my father returned to the truck, the dog was acting funny, and that was when I found out it was a spotted skunk.

My father was not impressed. Our hunting dog was not impressed. I was bathed in tomato juice and my coat was buried in the back yard. It was the only time I didn't have to eat what I shot. I did have to ride in the back of the truck.

There were times when I and my father would go into the swamps looking for small lakes to fish for big Blue Gill sunfish. The moss hanging from the Magnolia trees looked like grey gossamer hair and hung down to the ground for as far as the eye could see. Some of the Magnolia blossoms looked bigger than my head. The lakes were full of Cyprus stumps that looked like spears jutting out of the water. On one occasion, my father saw a huge Cottonmouth water moccasin snake floating out in the middle of a small lake. My father decided that he wanted that snake, so he got out his rifle and shot it. He almost cut the snakes head off. He then turned to me and said, go get that snake. The little dugout canoe was too small for him to go. There was no paddle so he cut a six foot branch for me to use as a paddle. I paddled that dugout canoe out to the middle of

that lake and lifted that three or four foot snake into the front of that six foot dugout canoe. Then the snake started to move toward me.

I knew that snake was dead. I knew that it could not hurt me. I had collected live snakes before. I still learned how fast I could paddle a six foot dugout canoe to shore Paddling backwards.

Another time, we were fishing under a bridge in a small pool of a stream. The scenery was always incredible, The Bridge was made off creosote planks and there was room under the bridge to fish standing up. The trees hung down over most of the water. My father was fishing for his favorite fish, which was blue gill sun fish. I had my cane pole and was fishing for minnows. I was on my hands and knees holding my line, all of a sudden the little pool literally seemed to explode as a southern pike grabbed the minnow and my hook. It headed out to the pond and I was just able to grab my cane pole before it went into the pond. I was actually able to catch that fish and I was a happy boy.

CHAPTER

TWENTY-FIVE

I preferred to be in the wild and wooly bayous of Gulfport, Mississippi. Most of the people I met and liked had darker skin than me. I was pretty dark myself. I was actually brown as a nut. I have Grandmother of four Native American tribes, Choctaw, Chickasaw, Cherokee and Lakota Sioux. I tan to reddish brown. Whenever I was hunting or fishing, the dark-skinned people of the Bayous watched out for me even if I didn't want them to. I later found out that white kids were considered spoiled if they were not raised by the hired help. The hired help were usually the descendants of African American slaves. I was surprised to find out that amongst Negros

as they were respectfully called at that time, this was a tradition of the south. I never felt threatened by any of the people of the Bayou. It was there that I felt at peace. It became my comfort zone.

I was fishing for bluegill, under the bridge over the bayou, and a cotton mouth water moccasin was chewing on my bluegill perch I had on a stringer down by my feet. I was curious what the snake was going to do with a fish on a stringer. All of a sudden I was flying up the bank. One of the women had seen the snake and had grabbed me and thrown me to safety. I think it had scared her half to death and I was smart enough to thank her profusely.

It was very close to the same time when I was walking over the bridge. I saw a floating mass of vegetation, when I looked up I saw a seven foot Alligator Gar fish flying out of the water, it had a mouth that looked like two feet of teeth. The jaws snapped shut about two feet from me and it landed on the floating vegetation before it flopped back into the water. I don't know if it was after a bird or me, but at that time I

was only five feet tall. I was so excited by the spectacular display it never dawned on me that it could have been after me.

I feel it prudent to remember Barbra. She lived across the street and she was the daughter of the ports Ship Pilot. I used to go fishing with her father in the Gulf of Mexico, when he went to pilot ships into Gulfport. I know she liked me and I was too shy to let her know that I liked her too. She was walking home from the grocery store and was run over by a pickup truck and killed. I still think fondly of her in my memories. I still regret her passing. I later found out that I was such an imposing figure people would tell me people were dead so that I would stop looking for them. My sister later informed me that Barbara was still alive.

I actually saw an old alligator Gar called Old Grand dad. He had scales the size of coffee cup saucers and he moved between the salt water and the bayous. I saw him in the port water of Gulf Port, and as he rolled it was fascinating and beautiful, he was estimated to weigh more than three hundred pounds, and it looked like a

continuous row of enormous green scales, a row of armor. I saw a sea monster for real.

My father had been a fish butcher on the Mississippi river in Illinois as he was working his way through College and the local Deputies in Gulfport Mississippi, thought it would be funny to put an eighty five pound Alligator Gar on our door step. The joke was on them. We had a freezer and we ate fish steaks for a long time from that joke. It was outstanding. My father was an experienced fish butcher. He knew how to butcher all kinds of fish for all kinds of cultures. We ate all kinds of fish.

CHAPTER

TWENTY-SIX

One of the problems with moving around when you are a boy is the fighting to establish your position in the world. Every time we moved I had to prove that I couldn't be pushed around. I would leave for school an hour early and would usually be late. My father followed me to school one day and found that I had opponents on every block. I think we all enjoyed the wrestling matches. This lasted for five years until I met this big kid who knew how to box. After he knocked me down for the seventh time, he finally got tired of hitting me and walked away. I was lucky, he could have been mean, unfortunately it was totally my fault, and

I was the one who challenged him. I found out that boxing was not as fun as wrestling. I took the time to heal and started lifting weights and learned how to really fight.

My father bought me a one hundred and ten pound weight set. I followed all of the instructions, and by the sixth grade I was five foot two inches tall and weighed one hundred and twenty eight pounds. My bone and muscle density caused me to sink in salt water. This was about the time when my father told me to forget about college because he couldn't afford it. Viet-Nam was in its third year. I didn't have to be a fortune teller to know my future but I'm getting ahead of my story.

I don't know why my father told me I could not go to college. He may not have known about scholarships and such because he went to school on the G.I. bill. I do know that my life seemed to depend on doing what my father told me. He was always right. I did not see any purpose in school work. I saw no reason to aspire in public education. I began to study the brain candy that I liked. School was a waste of time.

I guess I have to talk about school. I did not like school. I had to fight all the way to class and all the way home. I was bored to tears until I got to recess where I got to fight for an hour until I was able to go back to class to be bored again. I was a very good reader. I read most of the biographies and auto biographies in the school library. I think it is funny that the book I remember most was a book called "Four Wheel Drift". They caught me reading library books instead of school books and kicked me out of the library.

I read every science fiction book I could get my hands on. I then went on to Edgar Rice Burroughs. Tarzan, John Carter of Mars to name a few. Andre Norton wrote a lot about communication by telepathy and her communication with the Animals of other worlds. Robert Hienland wrote "The Cat That Walked through Walls". I read more books in a week than most of the students read in a lifetime. I was extremely relieved when my father purchased the World Book Encyclopedia, The Popular Science Encyclopedia. I needed

reference Books and I took full advantage of them.

I learned an unusual fact at the University of Maine. The average child has a maximum attention span of fifteen minutes. Most boys should have physical and sports training as their primary form of education until age nine. All class time that extends longer than fifteen minutes is simply babysitting for all ages. Our children all need more physical education than classical busy work/babysitting. Our children need music training to give them a greater understanding of mathematics. If they learned to fish and hunt, they would learn to feed themselves instead of looking for handouts. I'm just saying.

CHAPTER

TWENTY-SEVEN

When my father got out of the bed after his injury in the offshore drilling incident we started hunting and fishing until he could find a job. We fished in any water and ate a lot of sunfish and bluegill. We ate rabbit, squirrel and turtles, finally he was able to afford a cast net and that changed our fishing from fresh water to salt water. We would go out in the gulf at night and gig flounder with a lantern. My father got a job as a Deputy Sheriff and if he was off during the day we went into the surf to catch mullet and flounder with the cast net.

My father would frequently come home with booze on his clothes from busting illegal alcohol

clubs. All bars were illegal, but if you were tall enough to put money on the bar, you could buy booze. I learned this with my Uncles, Mike and Marvin. We heard about a deep swamp bar and we drove out there and it was kind of spooky. It was a Tent with boards on barrels as a bar. My uncle bought a small bottle of booze and we got out of there. My uncle may have been fourteen.

My father and I would head out to the beach with a cast net. I had a gunny sack tied to my waist. We would wade out into the surf and cast the net over schools of mullet. We caught many species of fish with the mullet. My favorite was flounder, but we also caught croakers, sand trout and sting rays. We usually let the sting rays go.

My father and I would spend hours cleaning fish. We would butterfly Mullet while my mother was cooking red beans and rice. My father would get the broken banana stalks that they gave him for security work at the Port and place them in the kitchen to ripen. We cleaned enough fish and shucked enough oysters for a fish fry. Beans and rice, mustard and turnip greens, fried fish and fried oysters. Sometimes on payday we would get shrimp. You may ask why we did not know we had little money. I guess I really did not care. My father later remarked that he didn't know if he really liked the taste of fish, but he did like the taste of fried cornmeal. All of our fish had to be rolled in cornmeal and then fried.

This reminds me of the time my uncle Ray went with my father and I to go gig flounder. We passed some pylons where we saw some Sheep head fish feeding on barnacles. My father succeeded in gigging three of them, weighing about a pound apiece. I had them on a stringer and was following them. All of a sudden my father saw three sting rays around us. My uncle and I moved closer to my father. The fish on the line swam around behind my uncle and the fins stung him on the back of his leg. He screamed "my God Herb, they're on us!" and with that, he jumped up on my fathers' back. So there was my father, a lantern in one hand, a gig in the other, and two hundred and fifty pounds of Ray on his back, surrounded by sting rays. I tried not to laugh, but failed miserably. My father

and Uncle splashed around in the surf, with my father trying to get Ray off of his back and screaming "get off my back you big lummox", while my uncle kept screaming "my God Herb, they're on us, I've been hit". I think we scared the sting rays half to death.

My father and Uncle Ray would occasionally go on the evangelistic trail together. My father eventually made enough money to buy a small two-seater Piper Cub Airplane. One day as they were flying ice slide into the carburetor in the engine. He looked at Uncle Ray, his brother, and calmly stated "well Ray, I guess this is it," my father was just being ornery because he knew the heat from the engine would evaporate the water in the carburetor. The plane was light enough to glide to a safe landing but Ray didn't know that. It is very difficult to get on your hands and knees in a Piper Cub Airplane, but Ray succeeded with great prayers and wailing and his prayer was answered when my father turned the key and restarted the engine. What was a miracle to Ray was just another cruel joke by my father.

The joke was on my father. When the congregations found out that he owned an aircraft, they quit giving him love offering and he couldn't afford to maintain the aircraft. People seem to forget that most ministers have families to support as well as their congregations outreach and without tithes and offerings they have all the responsibility and none of the resources. A minister's lifestyle reflects the generosity and prosperity of their community.

CHAPTER

TWENTY-EIGHT

In Gulfport, Mississippi there is a breakwater that protects the fishing fleet from storms. It is about eighteen inches wide with two foot by four foot concrete cross beams every ten feet. It was my favorite place to fish. I wore out fishing poles catching trout and red fish there. The first time we went to the Breakwater in Gulfport, Mississippi, we didn't know how to fish for crabs, so my father attached a large gage fishhook to the end of a bamboo cane pole and he used it to hook crabs off of the pylons, rocks, docks and the side of the breakwater. I ate so much crab that I got sick of crab.

My father had a small fishing rod with braided nylon line. He had spotted a large redfish trapped behind the breakwater. He actually was successful in placing a hook into the mouth of that huge redfish. You had to see this to believe it. That fish must have weighed fifty pounds. My father had to know that there was no chance for him to keep it but he walked up and down the breakwater with that fish for at least an hour. The fish finally got annoyed with him and broke the line. The excitement of playing with that fish was worth the ridicule and humor of the moment.

The one thing that stood out in my memory was, shrimp for twenty five cents a pound, if you bought four pounds... Oysters could be purchased for a dollar per gunny sack. A gunny sack would fill up a bushel basket. You could buy a cheeseburger, fries and a milk shake for a dollar and get change back. Gasoline was twenty-one cents a gallon and during a gas war, I saw gasoline for seventeen cents a gallon. Minimum wage was seventy five cents an hour.

CHAPTER

TWENTY-NINE

I was out on the breakwater one day when a waterspout descended from the clouds about a hundred meters off the breakwater. We all had to grab the sides of the concrete to keep from being blown off. It scared us all half to death but we all survived the experience. It then started raining salt water.

My two Uncles, Mike and Marvin, went fishing with me occasionally, which was lucky for me, I was fishing and fell into deep water, that was when I found out that I could walk on the bottom without weights. My weight lifting had made my bones and muscle very dense. I was aware of everything in the Gulf, because

I was drowning. I remember the beautiful clarity of the water. I remember the pressure of the grab by Uncle Mike and then I awoke with them pumping the sea water out of my lungs. We went home for the first time without catching anything and all my Grandmother had was sweet potatoes baking in the oven, no fish for dinner. I didn't like sweet potatoes until I tasted them when I was really hungry, and they were pretty good. I know that I like butter and cinnamon.

When I wasn't fishing I was usually running the Bayou hunting snakes and lizards. I had captured twelve cotton mouth water moccasins and had them in a cage. My next door neighbor had been kicked in the head by a mule when he was a kid and they took out the bone but sewed the skin together and it was hard not to look at his head as his brain pulsed in the skin. I showed him my Water moccasins and he promptly reached into my cage and started draping them around his neck. That's when I met my first Pentecostal snake handler. I was fascinated but chocked it up to what can you

102

expect from someone that was kicked in the head by a Mule. I would never put a poisonous snake around my neck and would not recommend it to anyone.

We lived for a time in an abandoned restaurant at the airport that was donated to my father by members of the church, where he sang and led music with my mother, and she played the piano for my father.

My mother is one of the finest piano accompanists I have ever heard. My mother could change the song she was playing as my father changed the songs he was singing. My father would stop in the middle of a song and preach a while and then go back to the song, and then he would change songs. My father could sing and preach for what seemed an eternity to a twelve year old. I must honestly admit I didn't like Church even a little bit; I was bored out of my mind. The idea of spending eternity with the stodgy and controlling old farts in the Church was enough to scare me through and through. As an adult I suppose the thought of living eternally with likeminded people is a

good enough reason to experience the Euphoria of believing the love proclaimed by all of the people around you. There's a huge difference between instruction and righteousness and the Euphoria of mutual well-being. Children experience lessons in right and wrong and the art of correction and righteousness seems to be a rare talent. Most of the time, it is misunderstood by most children as nagging.

I know now that they were trying to direct me to a better life. It just seemed to me like they were all bullies.

We had a family experience with a man that had poor judgment with children. He took all the Preachers kids to a stag nudist film. Personally I thought it was pretty funny watching fat, dangly old people playing volleyball and jumping over hedges. The unfunny part that we did not know at the time was that he molested my little sister. She was so young that she thought the man was our father. Until the day she died, she believed, because of psychological transference, that my father had taken her to a stag film and had molested her. This mistaken identity, not only

destroyed her trust in our father, but made it very hard for her to have a normal childhood. Persons that molest children do not deserve to live in my opinion, and I know that Jesus Christ had a similar opinion. It would have been better if they had never been born.

I was at least four foot six at the time. I was the perfect height so that when I got a hug from the women at church, it usually resulted in my nose in their cleavage. For some reason I never learned to turn my head. I hope they all enjoyed it as much as me.

I helped my father divide the restaurant that the church gave my father into two bedrooms and a living room. I had my very own mop closet next to the shower room and the bathroom, both of which opened into my mop closet. It was also next to the kitchen where the waitresses would pick up food from the kitchen. I did not have any privacy.

I saw a movie called The Horrors of Dracula. The movie was a classic and it had a moment where Count Dracula materialized through a locked door. This had quite an effect on a young

boy that lived in a room with no door. The scariest thing next to my room was the screechy noise the huge cockroaches made as they slid across the pots and pans in the kitchen. My absolutely natural response was to go sleep in the living room with a radio next to my ear. I would turn on the swamp cooler and pull the blankets over my head, usually with my tom cat Boots curled up on my chest. That was the first time I heard an Elvis Presley song. It was the first time I wanted to sing in a style different from my father. Rock and roll was not listened to in our house.

CHAPTER

THIRTY

My parents failed to tell me that they were going to move the house from the airport to a new lot in Gulfport close to Westside Junior high, and when I came home from school one day the house was gone, they tried to move my cat Boots in a bushel basket with a screen over the top but he clawed out of the basket leaving me and my tom cat alone in an empty lot. The tom cat was waiting for me as I got off the bus. He went home with me with no problem. I knew they would pick me up eventually, but I kind of wished they would have told me in advance, or where they moved the house. Moving that house seemed to be quite traumatic, but it was

a relief to get it on a piece of property we could call our own.

My cat Boots was born in Gulfport Mississippi, around the time of my fathers accident. Boots for some unknowable reason, liked to sleep in the doorway until my father stepped on his tail. Boots had a broken tail all of his life. He never trusted my father for some reason. Boots liked to sleep on my chest. The habit of sleeping on my chest was enjoyable to both of us. There was only one problem, if someone he did not know walked through the front door, he would dig all twenty claws in my chest as he sprang to safety under the couch. It made me be very watchful of strangers.

CHAPTER

THIRTY-ONE

The Switzer family was especially close to us and on Sunday morning Cal Switzer would bring donuts; which was very thoughtful. Once he brought black eyed peas and hog jowl, said it was a tradition of the south to eat these on new tears day. One thing my mother didn't like was chicory in her coffee. Even when you bought regular coffee, it seemed like the local venders put in a little chicory as a regional flavor enhancement. In the New Orleans French Quarter they served chicory coffee with equal parts hot cream poured from large silver coffee pots and that was a treat, but it never turned out just right at home. One thing was a constant,

my mother loves her some coffee. My father Herb had a good opportunity for ministry in the church with music. He actually had two radio broadcasts that were provided by the radio stations so they could provide religious services without having to ask for funding from the audience.

We were very naive about the racial situation when we moved to Gulfport, Mississippi. We knew there were separate bathroom facilities for blacks and white also separate drinking fountains for blacks and white. We just didn't know the meaning of black. If you were any color but white, you were black. People were so divided, that cultures didn't associate with each other and were able to close their eyes to the suffering of others outside their race. It was against the law for blacks to go to white assemblies/churches.

Consequently our church was all white. There were no blacks on the beaches except for a small area and there were no whites in that area. There was 29 miles of manmade beach between Biloxi, Mississippi and New Orleans,

Louisiana. Do you think that all entire beaches were built by white people?

My parents were involved in a real clash of culture and law when two men from India, who were to minister in the Revival Center, They would have been insulted if they were put up in a black hotel or motel because they didn't consider themselves black either. We could not put them in a white motel because it was against the law and my father was also a police officer. The pastor, Garland Pemberton asked my parents to let them stay at our house.

We had a small house but we had a two bedroom trailer beside our house that Ray and Doris had previously lived in. My father of course, said "bring them on in, its fine for them to stay there". The women of the church prepared for them by bringing in food and served it to them in our home. People were very upset about us letting those men stay in our house. They drove over our garbage cans but because dad was a policeman, they only objected verbally. I don't remember much about those men, the women of the church were astonished when they ate

two raw eggs before they ate breakfast. They spoke very good English and were a blessing to the church, the traditions in the south made it difficult and it was easy to reach an impasse in every aspect of life. Control is only an illusion.

My mother was especially embarrassed when a black man came to our door and asked if the restaurant next door would serve him coffee and my mother of course said "I don't see why not". They wouldn't serve him in the restaurant but did serve him in his own cup from the side door. This is especially funny when you realized that the people that owned the restaurant were Italian and they were considered black too.

My mother used to brag that we didn't have any race problems in the Rogue Valley, Oregon where she grew up until years later when she found out that they had a Jim Crow Law in Medford, Oregon for years. That meant that a black person was not allowed to stay overnight in the area. My mother had in fact, never seen many black people until the Government sent in black soldiers to build Camp White. I guess it is possible to ignore what is around you if the

races are so divided that you can live in ignorant bliss while serving your community and church. I guess ignorance is bliss.

Grandma Louise, Uncles Mike and Marvin moved to Gulfport, Mississippi and lived in an apartment on the beach. Can you imagine what the people would have thought if they had known she was a half-breed Native American? We would all help out when we could but none of us were doing too well financially. There was always plenty of fish. There is never any such thing such as extra money!

CHAPTER

THIRTY-TWO

The move to a new lot was unique in that I had to dig a septic tank hole by hand, of course the majority of the work was done by my father, but it seemed an eternity before we got it done. We then had to build a chicken house for our ducks and chickens.

I eventually got back to fishing on the break water. I saw a guy trying to catch white trout with fancy fishing gear. I politely informed him that there was a simpler way to catch the fish. I was catching trout at a rate of four to his one. I allowed the tide to move my bait and used cut mullet for bait. I was surprised to find that he was the local sports editor and he wrote me

up in the local newspaper. Then along came Hurricane Betsy.

We had just finished the house when Hurricane Betsy hit Gulfport, Mississippi. It was great fun to fall forward and let the wind pick us back up, that was until the wind blew half of our roof off. We hunkered down until the Hurricane went by. Then as we were watching a dark cloud was moving in from the Ship Islands. It was mosquitoes. There were so many mosquitoes that it looked like the lawn lifted up to meet us. We would rub our arms and the dead mosquitoes looked like an oil slick on our arms. The DDT fog from the trucks was the only safe place outside, so we played in the fog of the Mosquito trucks.

Martin Luther King tried to put his daughter in a white school, the atmosphere was too angry to remain in Gulfport. Mrs. King took her daughter and left Dr. King to sort out the situation and to protect their daughter. The community had bought up all of the guns and ammunitions in order to fight against segregation. My father was a police man and he

decided that the situation was too dangerous for his children to be involved, and at that time we moved to Arden, Nevada; where by the way, they don't have Hurricanes or Tornadoes.

We moved to Corpus Christy, Texas, just in time for Hurricane Carla. After Hurricane Carla, my mother asked my father where there were no Hurricanes or Tornadoes. My fathers' brother was the dispatcher in Arden, Nevada. That is how and why we moved to southern Nevada, ten miles west of Las Vegas, Nevada.

CHAPTER

THIRTY-THREE

We moved to Arden, Nevada which was 10 miles outside of Las Vegas, Nevada in 1963. The desert is so different from any place we had lived at that time but all of us reveled in the open spaces and freedom of movement. The Mojave Desert is one of the deadly places on earth and without water; you can die within 24 hours. That's pretty dry.

I seemed to be unable to change my ways and I would strap on my knives and go out into the Mojave Desert and hunt lizards. I would drink water from barrel cactus. I would cook lizards over a sagebrush fire and eat them. Instead of swinging through the trees on honeysuckle

vines, like I did in Mississippi, I would drag car hoods up the shale slide hills and slide down the shale like snow. I could survive. I was thirteen.

Arden, Nevada was a very small railroad community with several local characters who were squatting on the railroad property around the Depot and tracks. There was a large cement slab that we children played on but the sidewinder rattle snakes liked the warmth of the slab too. Skating with rattle snakes, we learned to watch out for hidden dangers and miraculously no one was injured or bitten even though they ran through the desert looking for lizards and colored glass from the years of drunken railroad bums tossing their bottles. There were a lot of bumps and bruises, but that is normal for our age.

We moved in with Uncle Bob and Aunt Ann and they had seven kids of their own. My mom and dad had 5 kids. 16 people in all make a large house very small in a short time. Make no mistake it was a very loving time, but close. They had a large house there and uncle Bob worked as station manager at the depot. My

dad got a job working on the railroad with the Native American Mexicans because he had to have six months residency before he could be hired as a deputy Sheriff. We moved into an old run down house near the depot that was condemned. There was no electricity and nothing worked but it was nice to get out of the bedlam and close quarters at the big house. It is difficult for two large families to live in close quarters. My uncle Bob and Aunt Ann were quite gracious about the whole thing and we thanked the Lord for them.

I was still one of the smallest kids in school. I and this other dark skinned fellow used to fight each other all the time just to keep the bigger kids from picking on us. It actually worked. I guess it is not fun to pick on people that seem to like fighting all the time. Chest pumping is not as much fun if you have to back it up.

My father was working on the Union Pacific railroad with a group of Indians from Chihuahua, Mexico. They taught us how to make green chili and tamales. I still make them. I went hunting Deer with them and they supplied the

food and water, which consisted of ten bean burritos, fifty jalapeno and beef burritos, and a gallon of whisky, no water. After the first day, the bean burritos were gone. I had never tasted whisky or jalapenos before and after the third day I felt as though I could set the sage brush on fire with a single fart. I was miserable. By the fifth day I was feeling macho. It is amazing what you can get used to if you have no choice.

People would go deer hunting and out of the goodness of their heart, bring their deer to feed our families. I think we butchered 5 deer while we were staying there in Arden, Nevada. My father and I found Lake Meade and we used to catch literally hundreds of Crappie under the lights at a dock my father had permission to fish at night. Of course we also caught hybridized Stripper, Large Mouth Bass and sunfish. The Lord provided all that we needed as long as we went out to harvest the local bounty. The Lord helps them that help themselves.

My father and Uncle Bob used to make extra money by unloading box cars when the loads got messed up. They would restack pallets of cement. The bags used to weigh one hundred pounds each. My cousin was even smaller than I was. He was Five foot four when he graduated high school. He was eventually five foot ten a few years later. We worked our little behinds off. Then a one armed guy showed up and he carried two bags at a time. He would throw them on the pallet and stack them. The two of us, my cousin and I could not keep up with him.

The railroad permitted us to move into the living quarters in the back of the Dispatchers office and it was much more comfortable even though we were still quite crowded.

Walking through the desert I chanced upon a couple living in a ravine. They had chanced upon a small seep of water from the side of the ravine. They made a roof out of tin over the ravine and channeled water to run through burlap bags and had an evaporated cooler of sorts. It was cool even in one hundred plus temperatures. They made pets out of the native snakes and lizards. I thought it was really cool, no pun intended.

One of the neighbors gave Patty a Siamese cat. It wouldn't eat anything except raw eggs with canned milk and sugar. It would not let my dad sleep during the day and my father was working grave yard. The cat would jump right up on my fathers' chest and yowl in his face. I once saw that cat trying to grab hold of the wall because my dad had thrown it off the bed. Twenty claw scratches all the way down the fresh painted wall. It really broke Patty's heart when she had to return that cat, tears flowed like rain.

Arden, Nevada is where I had my first motorcycle. It was called a Harley Topper. It had an eighty horse power engine with a centrifugal clutch. It would actually hit eighty miles per hour on the Highway. One of the problems with living in the foothills of the mountains is washouts. The roads can washout because it rains in the mountain and the flash floods wipe out perfectly good roads. I was going ridiculously fast when I saw a twelve foot section of the road six feet deep washed out. I was going

fast enough to make it to the other side, but my Harley was two feet shorter. I buried it in place.

I had a friend that was an expert in reloading ammunition. He owned a twenty millimeter cannon which he had mounted in a little red wagon. It fired with a lanyard. It was fun to kill the hill. My father got a job as a deputy sheriff and he didn't want to live in the city of Las Vegas and thought we would be more comfortable in one of the outlying communities, we moved to Mount Charleston, Nevada because there was a large trailer/mobile home to live in. Mount Charleston is a beautiful place to live in and visit.

CHAPTER

THIRTY-FOUR

I was in High School and my father was a Deputy Sherriff at Mount Charleston. We actually lived in a Sheriff Sub Station. It was really cool, because our friends were the crazy-assed firemen. One of them used to eat moths by the flickering firelight. It's amazing what you remember as a young teenager. We had a mobile home furnished by the Clark County Sheriffs' department. The mobile home was not grounded properly so we kids would hold hands waiting for some unsuspected victim to come along. We would invite them to play along and as soon as they grabbed our hand, the kid on the other end would grab the metal handrail and it

would shock the crap out of the new kid. If they cried they were invited to help play the trick on the next kid. They always wanted to share the experience with someone new.

I and two friends were the Teenage Mountain Men. We would hike all over Mount Charleston. When it was time to come home my friends' mother would yodel, and we could hear her in the clear mountain air. We were headed to the tree line, but realized we were a little late so we left the trail to take a short cut home. We knew we were headed in the right direction, because we periodically heard a yodel. It was just starting to get dark, when we started down Mary Jane Falls. When it got too dark to climb, we found a ledge with a hollowed out log. We built a fire, and took turns getting warm in the side of the log. We used the wood from the fire side of the log until we had a comfortable warm place to curl up in. It gets cold at night in the Mountains. We were all dressed in shorts and T shirts. We were actually quite safe. We were followed by two Mountain Lions that met at the top of the Mary Jane Falls. They proceeded to fight each

other for half the night or so it seemed, when my father showed up at the bottom of the falls in his Patrol car. He spotted us with his spot light and spoke to us with his loud speaker. He agreed with us it would be safer to climb down in the morning. Somewhere in the night someone was laughing hysterically. Between my father, the Mountain Lions and the crazy dude, we didn't get much sleep that night. To make matters worse, the incident was written up in the local newspaper. The lesson learned, "so much for short cuts".

CHAPTER

THIRTY-FIVE

The next summer I worked in Mount Charleston for a trail ride. I helped a girl take people on trial rides. We fed and groomed the horses. The girl had a man hating horse. They were quite a pair. She and her horse seemed to have the same attitude. We would take the stake bed truck down a dirt road to Pahrump, Nevada to pick up hay. The three strand bales weighed on the average one hundred and fifty pounds. I had never seen alfalfa bales so heavy. Most of the hay I had seen weighed sixty to seventy pounds. It was hard work but I learned to enjoy it.

CHAPTER

THIRTY-SIX

The Sheriffs' office was in the process of establishing a substation in Indian Springs, Nevada and asked my father if he would be interested in going to Indian Springs. They didn't have the Sheriffs sub-station built yet so they put us up in a mobile home in a mobile home park until the Sub-Station was ready for us to move into. It was a small one-bedroom mobile home and there were 7 of us. It was the summertime and there was a nice swimming pool so my parents thought we would survive it. We were there longer than expected because it took longer than expected for them to get the sub-station finished and ready to move into. We

the children slept on the floor and my father would have to step over us when he got a call for some police emergency.

I cannot tell you the Joy of moving to a new town, when you're the smallest guy in your grade. It is just as bad to be the son of a police officer, and even worse to be the Preachers kid. Needless to say, I was all of this and more. Nobody ever passed up on the opportunity to try to get me in trouble. I used to tell people that I couldn't even think about doing anything wrong.

Riding horses became my popular pastime, because my sister got a Quarter horse gelding. I got to ride a horse that was a stand in for Trigger in the movies. That Palomino taught me to ride. If you pulled back on the reins he would come to a sliding stop, and if you pulled on the reins twice he would stop and do the classic rare up, the one that you saw Trigger do in the Roy Rogers Show. It was all worth it, even the sore rump it caused, until I learned how to ride him.

I rode horses and motorcycles at the gravel pit. Mostly we rode dirt bikes. I always had to

borrow some ones bike. One day I was driving a fifty cc Honda when the front tire became caught in the deep powder and flipped us into the air. I landed face down in the dirt, the guy riding behind me, landed on me, then the bike landed on him.

I learned the basics of making life sized dolls from my aunt and of course we made a life sized cowboy and hung him with a hang mans' noose at the gymkhana arena. The shock and awe, we thought it was so funny. It was a little funny.

When you are fourteen you do everything wrong, whether you plan it or not. We knew that the underage curfew was 10:00pm until 6:00am, but we still thought we could get away with it when we were supposed to be camping; we instead hitchhiked to Las Vegas. We went to an all-night theater and watched "Where the Boys Are" and the "Banana Splits" all night. There can be no worse punishment than having to watch that movie more than once. We couldn't stand it so we tried to hitchhike home at five- thirty in the morning. We got arrested for being out too early. We never thought about

the early curfew and they called my father to come pick us up. That was the last time I was beaten with a police belt.

My father of course had to inform me that he was responsible for bringing me into the world and he would be responsible enough to take me out of this world if I embarrassed him. What does that mean? I of course couldn't guess what would embarrass him so much that he would kill me. I just believed him.

CHAPTER

★

THIRTY-SEVEN

Once my dad had an incident where he had to arrest young man who was resisting arrest in the back of his patrol car and someone grabbed his service revolver holster and all and told him to let the kid go. It was of course very embarrassing for him and very dangerous because he knew the people he was dealing with and had not expected them to act like that. The next morning was a Sunday and my mother found the revolver thrown on the lawn. In a mobile home park there are a lot of small children running around the place and it was just the grace of God that no child had picked it up because it was still loaded. My father got a

new rig that didn't have a snap on hinge for the holster. It didn't take long for the family to get arrested along with all parties involved.

CHAPTER

THIRTY-EIGHT

Our dog Shorty was a Heinz variety, his mother was a Boston Bull terrier and his father was a Weiner dog, German shepherd mix. His sire looked like a short legged shepherd. Shorty was a black and tan and as ugly as he could be. The girls all loved him to death. He went to the laundry room and pissed all over a clean basket of clothes. The woman had no sense of humor and had to wash her clothes all over again. We had to give Shorty back to Uncle Bob and Aunt Ann and he remained with them for the rest of his days. When we finally were able to move into the sub-station, the first

piece of furniture was a Piano from Madeline Gartland.

CHAPTER
★

THIRTY-NINE

Indian Springs, Nevada is only a few miles from the Mercury Test site and the people that live there were mostly workers from the test site. Most people lived in mobile homes which were located in mobile home parks. Most of the homes that were permanent were on the land of the Air Force base. My Eagle Scout Master was in the Air Force and was from Hawaii. His name was Cocoa/ kahiliilioouakilani. We settled for Cocoa.

I became sort of a car buff. I worked at the Cactus Springs Service station when gas stations were still full service. We made commissions when we sold oil and antifreeze and such. We

gave a full inspection of all the car needs because it paid us to find a need to fulfill. Cars never ran out of fluids around us.

The manager of the Cactus Springs service Station ran a go cart with two ten horse power McCullough chain saw motors. It was clocked on the track at one hundred and sixty miles per hour. But it was one inch above the track.

The vehicle I liked was the dune buggy. There was only eighteen inched between the front and rear tires. The gas tank was a fifty five gallon barrel. It had a two eighty-three Chevy V- 8 with a duo-glide automatic transmission. We had to peg the throttle at half throttle in order to keep it from flipping over. It had roll bars front to back. We had to use Cadillac tires ballooned out on welded rims. It was a bomb, but we loved it.

We were a somewhat rowdy bunch when it came to cars and the desert. Somehow we had an old Desoto that was missing most of the body and roof. We were running down a dirt road with six of us in the car, we were going about fifty miles per hour. The steering wheel

came off. Joe looked at me and calmly said "here, you drive" he handed me the steering wheel as we plowed into the side of a ravine. We were laughing so hard, that none of us was hurt. When you are young you get away with a lot of stupid things.

One of my best friends had purchased a 1957 Chevy. We decided to put a large block three ninety-two Desoto V-8 Hemi with a push button transmission. When we got the engine and transmission in the car the drive line was only six inches long. The owner got into the car and made the mistake of putting it in reverse. He thought he would be going forward and the G-force pushed him into the throttle. He hit a telephone pole in reverse and totaled the car. We never got to ride in the car after six months of working on it.

CHAPTER

FORTY

My friends and I used to love to grill round steaks with sugar on them. We also heard that you could light a fart. We found out that this was true, but you had to wear blue jeans. If you wore loose knit Polyester the flames could go through the fabric and burn your ass. They even told a story of an Air Force pilot that got drunk and tried to light a fart in the cockpit of his Jet. He forgot to wear pants and caught his pubes on fire; the explanation to the flight surgeon must have been quite funny.

This leads to one of the most tragic events in my life at that time. I was sitting at home at the sub-station when my friends little brother

appeared at the door and told me that he had just shot his brother in the face with a four ten shotgun. I ran to the house and went into the parents' bedroom and I found my friend unconscious on the bed. I checked his vitals and he was breathing and his heart was beating. We tried to get an ambulance from the Air base, but we couldn't get through, so I ran to the airbase a half a mile away. I convinced them to come and check him out, but he died in the ambulance. When we talked to the little brother we found out it had been an argument over a wallet. The younger brother had loaded a four ten shotgun, but had pushed the cartridge under the bolt to make it look like he was putting a round in the chamber. He was arguing with his brother when his buddy thinking he would unload the gun, accidentally put the round in the chamber, thinking he was unloading the gun. The little brother told him that if he didn't give him his wallet he would shoot him in the face. He counted to three and shot his brother, my friend, in the face.

FORTY-ONE

My little brother Kevin was born June 2, 1966 while we were in Indian Springs, Nevada. My mother' doctor was in Las Vegas 43 miles away and he did all the physicals for the Sheriff's department. Dr. Potter was a private physician and delivered babies because he delivered Kevin in the Rose DeLima Hospital in Henderson Nevada and that was 60 miles from Indian Springs. Because my little sister Becky had delivered very fast, the doctor told my mother to come in and he induced labor. It was a difficult labor and he gave my mom a spinal and Kevin was born. A nun took Kevin away so fast that it worried my mom but the

reason she took him away was because my mom needed corrective surgery. That nun was always in charge of the newborns and no one challenged her. When my father saw Kevin he was trying to rub a spot off of his chest until he realized it was a mole. Dad called his mother Louise in Las Vegas and said he was going to call him Kevin Muldoon, but calmer minds intervened and his middle name is William.

My father started to bring me along on accident calls shortly after that, because I started to grow up, I guess. We went to an accident on the Lee Canyon road. A guy had driven a Triumph seven down the road at an estimated one hundred and fifty miles an hour. He went a hundred feet, before he hit a cactus and flipped over. He lost his roll bars that had only been spot welded on, and lost his head along the way, the car continued on for eighty feet, hit another cactus and stopped fifty feet further along and landed on its wheels. The symbol on the side of the car was a Road Runner with the words beep, beep, and my ass. My father thought I should witness the satire.

CHAPTER

FORTY-TWO

I was working out in high school so I could go out for football and wrestling in my senior year. I was getting very strong and maybe a little cocky. One day my father told me to go mow the lawn. I told him I had more important things to do. He grabbed my shirt and lifted me six inches off the floor with his weak left arm. As I looked him in the eye, he said, "What did you say to me?" This gave me a moment to reflect. He was not straining. He was holding one hundred and seventy five pounds, no sweat. I looked him straight in the eye and said "I said I'm going out to mow the lawn sir." He put me down on the floor and said "I thought that was

what you said." I immediately went outside and mowed the lawn.

CHAPTER

★

FORTY-THREE

I graduated from Bayou View Elementary School in Gulfport, Mississippi. I graduated from Western High School in Las Vegas, Nevada, 1968.

I started training for football in my junior year and my sister Linda took over my paper route and learned to drive. It was a challenge in the early mornings delivering papers and learning to drive at the same time. Mom says they got rid of the paper route as soon as they could find someone to take over the route.

We moved into Las Vegas, Nevada in time for my senior year. I had just started to grow my junior year. I grew from five feet two inches

and one hundred and twenty eight pounds, to five foot ten and one hundred and seventy five pounds in three months. It took me my junior year to get in shape for the football team. My strength and coordination had to follow my growth spurt. After training for an entire year I was still one hundred and seventy five pounds. The difference was a distribution of muscle mass. The summer of 1967 we moved to Las Vegas, Nevada in time for my senior year.

When we moved to Las Vegas my parents decided to buy a new home. I was riding a school bus 43 miles each way or if I missed the bus I would drive my car. It was almost impossible for my parents to think of the kids spending all that time on a school bus. If they had known about our experiences hitch hiking in the supercharged cars, they would have moved sooner. I remember going 43 miles in about fifteen minutes, the car was balanced and blue printed and had a buzzer that told you to slow down. The buzzer was set on the last peg and buzzed all the way to Las Vegas; we were going close to two hundred miles pr. Hour. We got a

ride one time in a Dodge 383. There is a quarter mile, 45 degree turn coming into Indian Springs and she was going so fast that the wheels were squealing all the way around that turn. I had a 57 dodge station wagon, with a 350 v8. It was red and white two toned with the highest fins of any car at that time. My friend Dusty Weed had a Triumph 650 one of the fastest street bikes of the time. Riding to Las Vegas would numb the entire front of your body, especially your face. We didn't wear helmets until a biker came in with a Great Horned Beatle imbedded in the face mask of his helmet. That bug was as big as a fist and it was flying! Nevada is one of the finest places to ride motorcycles, but it also grows giant Beatles every 5 to 8 years. Those bugs can really hurt you.

FORTY-FOUR

My father didn't want to buy a house but all they had to pay was closing costs. We didn't have to put any money down so they bought a three-bedroom house near Western High School. Mom says the house cost $16,000. The monthly payment was $130 per month and that seemed overwhelming at the time. It was a comfortable brick home and we had really good neighbors but because it is a transient town, it took a long time to get to know them.

The high school was in quite a lot of turmoil because of the race riots. There were drive by shootings; the Cowboys were cutting off the Hippies' long hair in vans with sheep shears. If

your hair was long enough to grab it was too long. The Huns used to do the same things to their enemies with the exception; the Huns would drag you across their saddle and cut your throat.

The police were constantly checking the Cowboys because their chewing tobacco tins were used by the Hippies and they, the Hippies, sold drugs in those same shaped tins.

During the race riots a group of black students stopped me in the hall and told me I had really big arms and asked if I knew how to use them. I informed them that I was the 191 weight class Varsity Wrestler of the High School. They let go of my arm and said they were just checking. Don't you just love a sense of humor? It was a very dangerous time.

FORTY-FIVE

My friends by this time we mostly involved with the high school rodeos. We had a bucking barrel made out of a 55-gallon barrel. The barrel had four cables with one ton truck springs attached to four pylons in a square. We could use it for bull riding or bareback and saddle bronco practice. No animal could buck as hard as that barrel. We usually only had one person on the cables because the more people you had on the cables, the higher you went up in the air. If the barrel went ten feet up in the air and you came off the barrel, you went up while the barrel went down. If you went high enough the barrel came back up to meet you. We drank

Coors by the quart at these events. You drank one quart before you rode and at least one more after.

CHAPTER

FORTY-SIX

We went to most of the local rodeos and in Nevada that meant anything within 300 miles of Las Vegas. I somehow never had the entry fee, so I usually worked the gates. We went to Alamo, Nevada for a jackpot rodeo. A California cowboy was mouthing off about how much better he was, so one of the guys put coarse sandpaper around a broomstick and dipped it in kerosene. As the California cowboy left the gate he pulled the bulls' tail across the broomstick. They also used a cattle prod to the flank of the bull. That bull exploded out of that gate like he was shot out of a gun. We thought

that bull was going to kill him, but we saved him. He never shot his mouth off again.

I grew fond of working the gates. I worked the gates at Mesquite and other small rodeos and gymkhanas. Gymkhanas are equestrian events where most of the cowgirls practiced barrel racing, they also ran pony express, donkey rides, and sheep races and greased pig competitions. It was a full day of family fun for all.

FORTY-SEVEN

My mother worked part of one year as a teachers' aid at Rose Warren School in the Kindergarten reading program. It was interesting but she decided if she was going to work she would prefer to get paid more for her time. My mother took the U.S. Postal exam and was hired right away. My mother is 5'2"tall and strong so they put her in parcel post and that job requires a lot of lifting, it is a real hard job. The men that she was working with were upset that women were getting the same wages as the men and they didn't think it was fair. That meant that the women had to unload trucks with the men and some of it was very

heavy. My mother transferred out of parcel post as soon as possible, she figured out that if she survived parcel post she could take anything the Post Office would dish out. She figured it couldn't get any more physical and she could handle it. My mother worked many jobs in the Post Office and liked working there with the exception of the Christmas season. She and the other employees; worked 11 hours a day, 7 days a week, She hardly recognized Christmas because the rush lasts until the middle of January.

FORTY-EIGHT

Hell week in Las Vegas is as close as you get to too hot to breathe. I put up with the heat and made the football team. I worked out until I was one hundred and ninety three. I would have played more if I had been college material at least that is what the coach told me. He wanted the guys that were scholarship bound to get exposure. I was a good second string player. I played defensive center and tackle. I do remember that I was hard to tackle, so the coach decided to give me a chance to run the ball. He told me to run right over the guard. I said do you want me to hit the hole in the line? He told me you run over the guard. I ran over

the guard and I didn't get to run the ball again. The Coach didn't think I was funny because I did literally what he told me to do.

Wrestling was a strange year. I had gone from one of the smallest kids to a kid larger and stronger than most. People did not search me out to fight anymore. We had a coach that had never wrestled before. We worked out and were trained by the kids that had wrestled years before. We did alright. I was having trouble making weight at one hundred and seventy five so my dad decided it was time for an old Indian recipe. He took some kind of tree bark and made me a cup of tea. This was in preparation for the zone tournament. I needed to lose three pounds; I lost eight ponds on the toilet. I was so weak I could hardly move. MY opponent had just popped a hernia. He was as weak as me. I lost six to four. He had four years of wrestling experience. I had one.

I didn't have wrestling experience, but I looked good. My neck and thigh muscles measured nineteen inches. My biceps were seventeen inches. My thigh muscles were thirty-four while

my waist was thirty-two. My chest was forty-eight inches. I won some matches just because I was so much stronger than my opponents. I eventually gained skills. I was working on Judo and Jujitsu. I was also working out in Karate. I actually graduated from High School with a B average. I lettered in football and wrestling.

CHAPTER

FORTY-NINE

I have a pet peeve. I call it wasted intellect when it applies to families in the Americas. I come from a long line of intellectuals, but my father informed me when I was twelve, that I could forget about College, because he could not afford it. I believed him and started lifting weights and learning how to fight. I took no particular interest in school, because there was no reason to do any effort on precollege course work. I was already reading five books a week until I was restricted from the library for reading non-school curriculum. I had read most of the World Book and Popular Science Encyclopedia.

My father was an Evangelist and a Deputy Sheriff and when he told you something, the only acceptable response was Hallelujah! At the age of twelve I was five feet tall and weighed about one hundred and twenty pounds.

I read all of Edgar Rice Burroughs books that I could find. I read the Doc Savage series and the Executioner. I also read every science fiction book I could get my hands on. By my senior year I was reading at least seven books a week, all of which was called brain candy. They gave us the Armed Forces Vocational Aptitude Battery, and afterward I was called into the Councilors office and berated for taking special education classes when I had some of the highest scores in the school. At this time I was five feet ten and weighed one hundred and ninety-three pounds most of that weight was muscle from working out all of those years, I was told that when I graduated from High School I was on my own.

CHAPTER

FIFTY

This of course leads up to my first construction job before going into the Marine Corps. We worked at the Mount Charleston Ski Lodge. We built the foundation for Garages by hand moving boulders to stabilize slopes for slabs. We operated an automatic lathe for all the staircases. We learned to finish concrete and at the end of our time found out we had worked for room and board because we did not have a signed contract for pay. He laughed at our ignorance and didn't even pay us minimum wage. He used to be a business partner of Howard Hughes or so he said. He and my father laughed because it was a lesson well learned. My buddy and I were

joining the Marine Corps together, but when my buddy went to the physical, he failed because he had a Testicle that he had not dropped, so I went into the Marine Corps broke and alone.

CHAPTER

FIFTY-ONE

I joined the United States Marine Corps in the first Marine Corps Nevada State Platoon in August of nineteen sixty-eight., I was supposed to become an avionics electrician. While in boot camp I was selected to become a Presidential Honor Guard, which resulted in them taking away my electronics schooling and the first time a lieutenant chose to pick me out of a line, placing me in the line of fire in the Infantry as a so called super grunt/mortar man. We lived in Quonset huts when we first arrived at M.C.R.D San Diego, California. It was otherwise known as "Boot camp". Yelling and screaming were the tone of the day until we understood the new

vocabulary. We at first had no idea what they were screaming about. Everything had a new name, if you called your rifle a gun, you had to run around the grid iron, screaming, "This is my rifle holding it with one hand, this is my gun holding your crotch, this is for fighting, this is for fun. If you had to go to the Bathroom, you had to run around the gridiron making siren noises for an emergence potty break.

I was given boots two sizes too small and was told to get them wet so they would stretch. I remember mopping the floor and the drill Instructor thought it was funny to throw a gallon of ammonia into our bleach and detergent. He then closed the door so we could experience chlorine gas in a closed environment.

Our platoon was the first to move into the new barracks. We packed everything into our duffle bags. We were making the move when someone tried to push me from behind. I lowered my shoulder, threw my duffle bag back and turned around to see my drill instructor on the ground, underneath my duffle bag. I prepared myself for an ass kicking. He hadn't announced

himself and to my surprise just told me to carry on. You would be amazed how quickly the drill instructors find places to punish recruits. The mop closet became an exorcize room where they could rant and rave at you in private and beat the crap out of you as long as it didn't leave any marks. They even stationed guards so they wouldn't be interrupted.

One private went into the office and told the drill sergeant he was gay. The drill sergeant stood up and pulled down his zipper and said, "I've been waiting for you to come forward for a month". The private hit the drill instructor with the butt of his rifle and jumped off the second floor balcony. We never saw the private again.

One of the privates cut his wrists in the shower. He failed to commit suicide so the rest of us had to sit through a class on how to commit suicide properly so we wouldn't waste the Marine Corps training time.

I was selected to go to Vietnamese language school at the Defense Language Institute West Coast in Monterey, California for a twelve week short course.

Language School is a very intense and difficult chore if you know you are going to Viet-Nam. If you fail you are going early. We had a very curious attitude. The question asked was, "What are they going to do, shave my head and send me to Viet-Nam." No matter what you did, you were eventually going to Vietnam. We all promptly fell in love with our instructor Co My. In Vietnamese that translates to Miss America. The joke was for us to figure out eventually. She was beautiful and nice, something we had not experienced much in boot camp and Infantry training. She had us wrapped around her little finger and she took advantage of us and taught us well. You had to be a combat veteran in order to be a Nixon era Honor Guard; you can guess where I was going.

Hello Viet Nam! I arrived in Viet Nam in June of nine-teen sixty-nine. (For your intimate knowledge I have included all of the letters I sent home from the military.)

Patty, Linda & mom

I am not the Platoon Leader. I was just the designated man in charge. I am not the Platoon Leader now.

I have been selected to go to school in Pensacola, Florida for communications after I get back from Boot leave. It is said that I will never get near the war zone (Vietnam). I will either be in communications or I will be an electronics engineer. That is the reason for the top security clearance. There were only 2 in our platoon selected and only 8 or 9 from all four platoons.

I am enjoying the Marines so far, but I haven't entered training yet. The Marines is much stricter than I expected in accordance with Patty's letter.

We start training Monday and we are here 8 weeks of training, I think I will be home for Christmas, I hope so anyway. Wow, this is more like school, we have

classes once or twice a day and will be having them every day. I have two religious classes every Sunday. Surprised?

Love
PFC Danny

Dear mom, dad &Family,

This information I am sending for is vital. I have been selected for Communications, for this job I have to have top secret clearance and I have to have all the information completely like I said. I have about six weeks to get all this information together and I have to get it from you.

We start training about tomorrow or the next day and it's not exactly fun but it's bearable. Don't be mad if I don't write very often, my time is going to be hard put.

Would you get Patty or Linda to call WENDY and get her address? Her phone number is xxx-xxx-xxxx Send that part to me with a word on how everything is going, and you have to send all the information to the address on the information sheet. I have enclosed. Please hurry on both replies.

I am getting to like Marine chow, but I especially like water. We shower and shave every night and have hygiene inspections. I got some different medications for the rash, but I think it's the wrong stuff because it doesn't do anything

Love always,
Danny

O&R Program Communications & Electronics Tech.

Education: list all schools I have attended since 9th grade, must have the complete name of the school, complete address, city, state & zip code.

Family: all members must have complete names including first, middle & last.

Mother: must have maiden name, complete birth place & birthdates for all family.

Permanent address: for all of the members of the family.

Employment: must have all jobs I have held that I have been paid for, the exact name of business or company, complete address zip code

of employer. For all jobs month, & year when I started and stopped, name of the immediate supervisor, first, middle & last (check on Jim Leck and Fred Bartby), reason for leaving, reason for quitting and all other reasons, (laid off etc.)

Credit & character references', credit - none established five character references, first name, middle name, & last name. Years known (over 2 years), exact business address where the references work, must have business zip code and city & state. (Bob Rajala, Bill Thornton, Jake Downs)

Residence: complete addresses of places I lived from D.O.B. 1950 to present, month & year I lived there, every place. Starting from 1960 all zip codes.

Get back all the information as soon as possible to this address.

National Agency Check Center, Recruit Classification, Marine Corp Recruit Depot (MCRD), San Diego, California, 92140.

Dear mom and dad,

I got the income tax return it came at the right time. I have to get stripes on my whole uniform and it is costing me $1.50 per shirt or jacket.

I'm trying to save money but it is almost impossible to save any.

Monterey is very expensive, the guys here that are married can't hardly afford to keep their wives here and its expensive to stay in a Hotel I guess, I don't think its half as expensive as Las Vegas.

I sure hope dad wins the tournament and I hope Bruce turns out to be a good caddy. How did you do it dad?

Tell Uncle Bob I said he'll be twice as disgusted with Idaho. Narcotics are as bad if not worse. I have a friend from the Midwest and them and told me about it. Las Vegas is bad but the kids at least always have something to do. This is not the same in California.

And if it's bad in California I can imagine what it will be like in Idaho.

When did Ellen get married? I didn't know about it. Well got to sign off, I'm finishing this letter in the dark.

Love always,
Danny

Dear mom, dad & Family,

I hate to say it but I miss Kevin as much as anybody and I wish I could say it. I miss all of you quite a bit when I have time to think of it. I am homesick but that will ease off when I'm too busy to think about it, today we worked for about 8 hours on unpacking and putting together beds, and it wasn't as easy as it sounds.

Well, what you think of me getting schooling. It's a pretty good break I think. The people or PUT's here are pretty good Joes. We haven't had any fights yet.

Had our bunk torn apart twice tonight because some idiot talked in the showers?

I have eight weeks or nine starting Monday, so I will be here a lot longer than I thought. From what I hear, the first three weeks of training is the hardest and we haven't even started training. Well things could be worse. I could have

waited till later to join. Write and tell me how everything is, good or bad.

I'm going to send you a Marine Corps Paper. (Hope you like it).

Hate to say it, but I have a Drill Instructor that I have a grave disliking for. But there's always one.

What really surprises me is that we get 1-3 cigarettes a day. Write back soon, don't forget to get the information and send me back the instruction I sent you so I can check it.

Love always
Danny

Dear mom & All,

I don't know for sure when I'm going to Graduate but I'll know two weeks before I graduate.

We go to the rifle range tomorrow bright and early. We'll ride in either a car or what they call a cattle car.

We have 1 week of only snapping in the following week we fire every day. You wouldn't believe some of the positions we have to get into. They are bad and it half kills you to get into them.

We have 24 training days left and Sundays don't count.

Well, sorry I wrote so much but it's about rack time. So Bye, Bye.

Love you all
Danny

Dear mom & dad,

How is everything? How are Kevin and Herbie? How is everybody doing? I'm doing pretty well, but I think I'm gaining weight. We haven't started our hardest phase of training yet, which is the Rifle range. Is the Dart an automatic or Standard? What year?

So far I don't dislike the Marines too bad. In fact, it's kind of fun.

There's a good bunch of guys in the platoon. We won the Academic streams today but we lost in drill. Our Platoon overall average was 83%. That's pretty good. (We got the highest overall average on the x1 test.)

Hate to always write so much but I can never think of anything worthwhile to say (lack of vocabulary) today was easy.

We had initial drill. We took the X-1 test, and we marched in a parade.

Well, gotta say bye.

Love you all,
Danny (PVTS)

Hi everybody, hope you have fun figuring out what I said. Yesterday I made Lance Corporal and I can't find any chevrons for my uniform.

I sure hope you all come up the 25th. I want to see you all before I leave here. I'm not enjoying Vietnamese; it's very hard to learn when we have to learn so fast.

Fishing ought to be pretty fair by the time you get up here and it will cost $9.00 a day. Now that you are totally confused will slow down and make sense.

I sure wish I knew what to write but I haven't written in so long I don't know what's going on.

Tell Linda, Patty, Becky and Herbie too write me and make sure you write me too. I want some letters. I will return all letters as fast as I can.

I'm getting awful dependent upon myself and USMC but, they don't make as

happy to hear from as you do. And tell the girls not to get mad if I don't write back within a week. I plan on starting to write quite a few letters now.

How is everything at home? How is the health of everyone holding out? Tell Linda and Patty to go on diets and Becky to eat more. Ha, Ha. Must go now.

Love always,
Danny

P.S. Don't anyone get mad at me just write and if anyone is mad tell them to write me and bawl me out.

P.P.S. Linda, tell Liz to write me, you too. Also, tell Jerry to write so I'll know their address.

P.P.P.P.S. Becky writes me. All your friends are too young.

P.P.P.P.P.S. Herby, write to me.

(TELL EVERYONE TO WRITE ME)

Boot camp; How do you explain Marine Corps Boot camp? I was carrying the Orders for the first Marine Corps Nevada State platoon. I was a category one mental group. I qualified for every High tech job in the military. I had a retired brigadier General telling them to send me to Annapolis. A lieutenant picked me out of line. He took away my schooling. He placed me

in the Infantry, which was my lowest aptitude even though my aptitude score was twenty nine points higher than I needed to qualify for the infantry. They told me someone intelligent had to lead the Infantry. Unfortunately they never passed that information to the dumb assed Officers they put in charge of me. I have a bad feeling about allowing someone else to have life and death authority over my life.

Those people have always disappointed me with their incompetence and their desire to place me in harmful situations without reason.

When we wanted to smoke, we had to yell out in unison "sir, the surgeon General had reported that Cigarettes are dangerous to your health. We don't care; we're going to die anyway. Light them up". If that doesn't say throw caution to the wind I don't know what does.

Boot camp is intentionally demeaning, unreasonably disrespectful, standing in line to be yelled at for no reason. With the explanation that if you cannot make it through boot camp, you are too weak and you would have broken under fire. They say they have to break you

down so they can build you up to be a Marine. I really wanted to punch people in the face for inferring that I needed help to become a man. My stomach muscles were so strong that they couldn't hurt me. They told me to act like it hurt so they could maul some other guy.

We had all kinds of people with all kinds of background. We had children of hairdressers to children of junkyard salvagers. One is no better than the other unless one has been taught to box. Mr. Manners only had to throw three punches to put down the junkyard dog. People decided to leave Mr. Manners alone. The moral of the story, if you have a soft spoken child, teach them or have your children taught martial arts.

Life is full of experiences that tell you not to trust anyone. It reminds me of a verse of scripture that states we must not place any one or thing between ourselves and the creator. The only thing you can count on is the fact that people will always take advantage of your trusting nature and stab you in the back. When you find someone that believes to live their lives

to love the Creator, love learning, and to do no harm and to do the right thing. Those are the people to Marry, the neighbors to cherish and keep close. This is the life work, to create paradise on earth. In my estimation, Paradise is in our relationships and not a geographical location.

People that call themselves atheists are sometimes quite intelligent, but why would you listen to a dead person. They take pride in their ignorance and puff themselves up like a toad. They are dead like a cow or a horse and why would you ask the livestock about salvation.

Without Jesus Christ all are dead in their sins and transgressions.

CHAPTER

FIFTY-TWO

My personal Armageddon occurred while I was in the Marine Corps in Viet-Nam. We were doing a security detail for the Sea Bee's. There is only one mined trail in the area and it is an old railroad track in an area we called Dodge City. It was one of the only times our Lieutenant went into the field with us. Our Lieutenant told us we had to secure the Railroad track. I informed him as a squad leader that we never used that trail because it was the only known mined trail in the area and that it would be suicide to walk on it. He informed me that I had a direct order to walk that trail or be shot for refusing a direct order in a combat situation.

I was the senior Lance Corporal Squad leader in my Platoon and was the only Squad leader to get my squad through my time as a Squad leader, without losing any men. I walked point and made it about two hundred yards before I experienced the concussion of two Grenades going off five feet behind me. The grenades had been buried in the gravel with a pressure sensitive trigger. Gravel makes it impossible to detect with the naked eye. The concussion blew me about sixteen feet forward and tore up my pack and flak jacket, which by the way saved my life. I was wounded in the side of my head, both arms, both legs and in my groin. My rifle was blown into two pieces. I was emergency Med-evacuee and was pulling shrapnel out of my penis and groin as they landed to pick me up. I was informed to layback down because I was an emergency medical evacuation. This was a successful alternative to having my Lieutenant be forced to shoot me in the head. I regret how much pain this caused my mother.

CHAPTER

FIFTY-THREE

My mother was alone in the house getting ready for work and a couple of Marines came to the door. My mother thought they only came when someone was dead, but they told her that I had been wounded, that I had stepped on a land mine and that my prognosis was good. Mom was really shook up when she got a telegram informing her of the same thing. She was only relieved when a ham radio operator relayed a phone call from me and she could hear my voice. I had a lot of shrapnel wounds but no broken bones.

I was in surgery, when I watched my monitor flat line. They could have let me go. They gave

me an adrenalin shot to stimulate my heart beat and brought me back. Someone had done my spinal block a little too high in my spine.

I awoke to the cleaning of my wounds. In Viet-Nam it is a very humid environment so they leave your surgery open in order to make sure that they get all infectious materials to show up before they stitch you up. This means they have to Butadiene scrub your wounds periodically to keep you sterile as possible. They sewed me up and I became infected anyway. They had forgotten the deep sutures and I developed cellulite in my right thigh.

I had progressed to the point of cleaning my own wounds. This involved taking long Q-tips and scrubbing out the seven inch gash in my right thigh. By removing the granuloma pus from the incision, it allowed the wound to heal from the bottom up. I was in the Hospital forty five days.

During my stay at the hospital I learned that the Lieutenant had lost two more valuable lives, trying to walk on that railroad track, and on the very same night he moved a listening post

without notifying the perimeter 106 recoilless rifle teams, which resulted in the death of my replacement sergeant and four of my squad members. I cannot swear to this because I was in the Hospital in DaNang. My Armageddon occurred when I decided to let go and let God. I decided to let the Lieutenant live.

I believe that Armageddon and jihad are interchangeable words that mean the same to me. When I have to choose the right path, or the evil path, I try to love the creator, love learning, chose to do the right and least damaging path, this is the choice between good and evil. Sometimes I win, sometimes I lose. If I fail, I have the right to apologize to the Creator and be forgiven. I can then continue on trying to get it right. *Try to love my fellow man and to be willing to put my life before theirs to protect and serve.*

When I went to Viet-Nam in June of 1969, I was kissed by the flight attendants and walked out into a world of burning kerosene and human waste I was loaded on to a truck filled with sand bags, to protect us from land mines on the road to the so called Riviera. Curiously there were

burning amphibious tracked vehicles on both sides of the road. There was only one person in the truck that was armed. This did not bode well for the future.

Dear mom and dad,

Sorry I couldn't write sooner but we've been out in the bush for 15 days. I had no writing gear so I couldn't write. If you could next time you send a package send some cigarettes.

Most of the guys are usually hurting for them so I usually don't have them. I've been played $50 dollars since I've been over here but the first of next month I will get paid. Today was the first hot meal I've had in 15 days. I've also got a case of emersion foot from being in the water so long, but it's not bad at all.

I've felt bad about not writing for the last week because I couldn't write anybody but I sure appreciated the letters.

One of our squads ambushed 4 VC two days ago but only killed 1, the others got away, but they think they wounded one other. I've been averaging about 3 hours of sleep a night because our platoon is

only half strength doing the work of a full strength platoon. We only have 35 counting all. We should have 50 at least. Our squad has 7 people.

Everybody pray for me. I'll be praying for you.

Love Always
Danny

Dear dad,

As in answer to your question; I have not done any hunting over here but there is a little wild game over here but from what I have seen, not much.

They have tigers and elephants and just about everything but not where I'm stationed.

They have a species of deer over here that looks about the size of two big jack rabbits or a medium sized dog. You can carry it under your arm.

They have a lot of fish and almost as much shrimp. I have seen fresh water shrimp 4 inches long with long pincers about 5 inches long. Looks more like a big spider than a shrimp.

They have a lot of snakes here, but all I have seen is the water snakes, the Bamboo Viper and the Vietnamese Rock Python. They have a Rock Python on display here

at the hospital 23 feet long and a smaller on 14 feet long.

Dad, what do you think of the police department would say to putting me through college? Forget that. When I get out of the service I am going to go to UNLV for four years but when I return to the States I am going to take college correspondence courses in English and History to get out my basic classes.

Don't lose that degree I got from Language School that is six or eight college credits. The reason I went into the service was to see if I could build a desire to learn and to study.

Now I have the desire to return to school I should be a pretty good student now that I know what I want.

Keep everything at home happy.

Love, your son
Danny

CHAPTER

FIFTY-FOUR

This leads up to an unusual sight of a burned wooden bathroom called a shitter. A Sergeant told a newly arrived Marine to go burn the shitter, when the private asked for clarification, the Sergeant replied for him to do what he was told without question, because in combat your life depends on quick compliance to orders. The Private promptly took the ten gallons of kerosene, poured it all over the building and set it on fire. For failing to give clear orders the Sergeant and the private had to rebuild the Bathroom. There was a unique smell of burning crap and kerosene. The Practice was to put Kerosene in a fifty-five-gallon half-barrel. You

placed them in the outhouse and periodically privates would be forced to pour kerosene into the barrels, set it on fire and stir the kerosene manure combination until it was burned down to ash. The entire country smelled like burning manure and kerosene.

CHAPTER

FIFTY-FIVE

When we arrived at our destination we found out that a platoon base called Bug Fuck Island, had been hit and that all available weapons had been buried and had to be recovered and cleaned before we could be issued a weapon. That night we were on the burm wall with nothing but bayonets. The next morning we found The Barber that had a straight razor to my neck the morning before, in the perimeter wire, with a satchel charge on his chest.

That night two 82 mm mortars' had landed in the movie area and luckily they were duds. Two of the people that had come in country

with me, received Purple Hearts the first night in country, due to shrapnel from the mortars that were not duds on the north end of the compound. We still did not have anything but a bayonet as we spent the rest of the night on the perimeter burm wall.

Dear mom & All,

It was sure good to talk to you over the phone but I'm sorry it's going to cost a lot, but it would have been four more days before I could have gotten a letter to you and I didn't want you to worry anymore. I would have called sooner or written sooner but I couldn't.

The wounds that are bad enough to mention aren't bad at all; two in right leg, calf and thigh, the one in my thigh was only an inch or two deep, the one in my calf about 1 inch, the one in left leg/ calf about % inch The one in my thigh /right leg got infected so it was reopened and is being cleaned up so it can be sewn up again. It will take about ten stitches; it's about 5 inches long.

I was a squad leader when I got hit. I stepped on a booby trap. I got 9 pieces of shrapnel in all but only three were bad

enough to cut out, the rest will work their way out in time.

I should be making Corporal pretty soon, but I'm not sure if I will or not.

Please do not worry further, I am alright. I even run already.

Thank you so much for the boxes. Please send fudge uncut.

Gods watch and keep all of you safe.

Love,
Danny

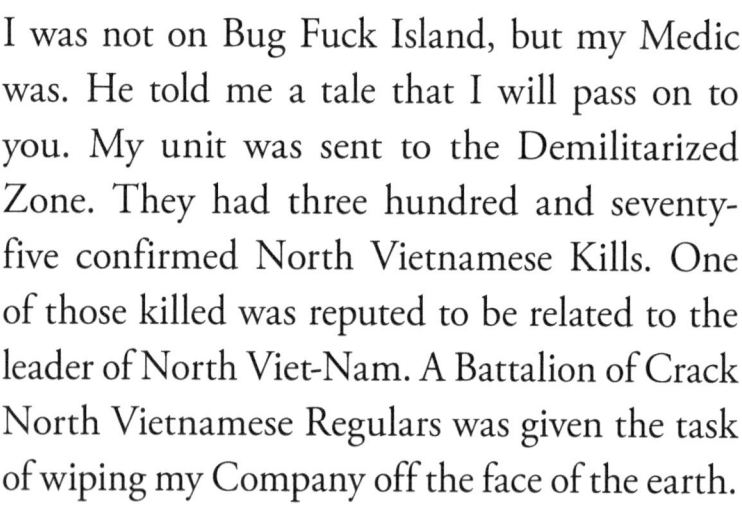

I was not on Bug Fuck Island, but my Medic was. He told me a tale that I will pass on to you. My unit was sent to the Demilitarized Zone. They had three hundred and seventy-five confirmed North Vietnamese Kills. One of those killed was reputed to be related to the leader of North Viet-Nam. A Battalion of Crack North Vietnamese Regulars was given the task of wiping my Company off the face of the earth.

Bug Fuck Island was the first retaliatory strike. Bug Fuck Island was a Platoon base.

The Platoon base was a sand bag built fortress. The number of a battalion of North Vietnamese outnumbered the Marines five to one. To most Marines, that means a fair fight. They somehow managed to overrun the Base, so the Platoon Leader sealed the remaining Marines in the Bunkers and Called in a barrage of Artillery in on their own position. Nine Marines were killed; the rest had to be dug out of their bunkers. This was a ferocious battle, by any standard. The Marines on that base were all seasoned combat Marines. I can only imagine the desperation that it takes to call an artillery strike on my position.

The same Battalion is the one that probed our Battalion on my first night in country. It took us a few days to clean up all the equipment from the Platoon base, but eventually we were issued our own rifles. We were also assigned to our Platoon and Squads, I was a Lance Corporal at that time and spoke a little of the language. I was soon issued an M-79 grenade launcher and

was kept close to the Squad leader. I carried Illumination, teargas, High explosive and shotgun ammunition and I spoke the language. I also carried a 45 caliber 1911-A1 pistol. I must confess. I really liked that pistol, even though you could not use the sights. The sights were so far off that if you aimed at one target you hit the target beside it. I learned to fire from the hip. It was so worn out that you did not want to shoot it at long distance. It was more a status symbol.

FIFTY-SIX

When we went on our first night ambush, two of our men were wounded and our Machine gunner was killed. One of the Marines went into the bush to take a dump and did not tell anybody that I know of. He farted and was shot three times. Another man was shot through the jaw. The machine gunner was shot through both lungs and died in my arms. We never knew where the shots came from. We suspected that someone had failed to notify the perimeter guards of the Naval Base, that there were Marines operating in their area of responsibility.

One night we were moving to an ambush somewhere along Highway one when we saw a firefight erupt about two thousand meters away. The man behind me was hit, and it looked like he had been sucker punched. When we rolled him over he was moaning and there was a fifty caliber round imbedded in his flak jacket lying sideways. Lucky for him it was a spent round from the firefight and it hit his Flak Jacket. If it had not tumbled and hit sideways, it would have killed him.

One of our units discovered an underground North Vietnamese Army Hospital with its blood supply donated by Berkley College along with Berkley College Sweatshirts. One of the captured Nurses was interrogated by our allies. The respect for human life is different in South Viet-Nam. We were ordered to observe and not to interfere. She was gang raped and questioned between rapes. She said nothing and was killed with a popup flare. I have had nightmares regularly about having to see something like that.

Dear mom & dad,

Just a line to say hi and that I am not a figment of your imagination. Thank you for the box, it was great in fact I think I have the greatest family in the world. Bar none.

Mom, send an informative list of what I bought. 163 days left in Nam. I should be home by graduation time. I sure do like oysters and clams smoked.

Dad, how is the fishing now and the hunting and the family. I sure hope everyone is fine. Tell Linda that letter she sent me about 5 months ago, if she'll send a letter with the questions I'll try my best to answer them.

Well, God Bless and keep you all, Merry Christmas.

Love
Danny

Dear mom,

How is everything at home? I am now back in the Bush; I still have my squad and I have been put up for Corporal although I don't know if I will get promoted. I should get it though.

My legs are in beautiful shape even if they don't look that way. You probably won't be able to see the scars by the time I get home.

Tell Linda and Patty if they don't write pretty soon, I'm going to be pissed off!

Please write Aunt Connie and tell her I have lost her address when I left the Hospital and I am not able to reply to the letters, also send my apologies.

Well, will go now.

Love and God Bless,
Danny

CHAPTER

FIFTY-SEVEN

I never allowed unusual cruelty by any of my Marines. We did not participate in the tactics of interrogation practiced by the South Vietnamese army because revenge rape seemed to be the norm in Viet-Nam.

Whenever a headman received aid from us, he was subjected to the rape of his daughters and was forced to watch. If he was caught again his head would be impaled in front of his house with his penis and testicles shoved in his mouth as a signal to the villagers, as a sign of what happens to anyone that aids or helps their enemy.

We had a man that played the movies in the Battalion rear. He drove to another base camp for movies. He hit a mine, but was still alive when the Viet Cong found him. They cut him a thousand times and he still crawled a hundred feet before he died. One of the squads caught a four man pay team. They tied them to the jeep. They carved 3/1 in their chest and put an ace of spades in their forehead. They then used the jeep for artillery practice. We never again found another man tortured while I was there.

Most days were boredom when you were on Bridge security. You always had to listen for rockets. One day we were alerted to rocket fire. The gunny was on the toilet when a rocket hit the toilet/outhouse. The building was totaled and when we ran up to the outhouse, there was the gunny, in the barrel with manure and kerosene up to his chin. Was it funny, yes it was, but we were most happy because he was alive and had not been harmed, with the exception of his pride?

When we got back to the main bunker we saw a guy sitting on the bunker with a rocket

sticking out in the air. He had been sitting cross legged on the bunker and the rocket landed between his legs and his crotch. He could not move. We had to un-wrap his body from the rocket that luckily was a dud. It failed to explode.

CHAPTER

★

FIFTY-EIGHT

My squad was involved in a search and destroy mission in some small village when one of the marines decided to pull a John Wayne. He pulled the pin out of a grenade with his teeth, which if you don't straighten out the pin, will break your teeth. He threw the grenade in the bunker and threw his back on the bunker. His problem was that he had thrown a grenade into the village latrine. The so called bunker was covered with Banana leaves with a bamboo frame. The grenade sunk all the way to the bottom and when it exploded it dumped all of the manure on him. He didn't get hurt, but he

did have to walk tail end Charlie all the way back to the base.

CHAPTER

FIFTY-NINE

No story of Viet-Nam is complete until you understand the intensity of the monsoons. Ninety-five degrees and constant rain, nobody moved around except us. The rice fields turned into a lake. When we had night patrols, we would set up on little hills and try to sleep in our ponchos. One night my poncho acted like a little boat and slid me ten feet down the hill that takes a lot of rain. We lost another Machine gunner to the monsoon, when the road broke and swept him away. He was carrying so much ammunition that we never found him until the water level lowered and we found him under

some roots under a tree, his machine gun ammo was still wrapped around his body.

The monsoon was a deadly time for the Vietnamese and we observed many dead bodies floating down the river from the floods. That is when they decided to spray Agent Orange on us and the river vegetation. The rains had stopped, so they gave the Agent Orange two weeks to work and then we went in with flame tanks to burn the dead vegetation.

We were on Bridge security, which involved shooting at large objects floating down the river. Some people, including a chaplain were able to come down and familiarize themselves by firing different weapons at mostly inanimate objects. Viet Cong were known to put explosives on bundles of twigs and try to float them to the Bridge in order to blow up the bridge. Sometimes you got a large explosion, sometimes it was a drowned human being from the monsoons. The Chaplain vomited when the object turned out to be a drowned woman he had been shooting at with a grenade launcher. We thought it was funny but thinking back on it, his reaction was

more normal. We had seen too many bodies floating down the river, so we were a little bit used to the experience.

CHAPTER

SIXTY

That reminds me of a newspaper reporter. He asked one of the young marines what do you feel when you kill a man. He replied, only the recoil of my rifle" and "the satisfaction of hitting my target" said another. In other words, the effect wears off after a period of times. Later we were told that the Hells' Angels sent our unit a letter saying we could join up without going through hazing upon our return state side. Who knows for sure?

We observed a party in the village next to our base camp so we set up an ambush in the last house at the end of the village. We placed the entire family in their cellar so they would

be safe along with our corpsman. We set up an L shaped ambush and settled in for the night. Four men with AK fifties walked out of the tree line into our ambush. We opened fire and they all went down. That's when we discovered that we had just ambushed a point element of a much larger unit. We suspected that it was the Battalion that was assigned to wipe us out. My squad was reinforced with an extra four men in a machine gun team. That meant I had twenty one men in all. We held the high ground with one hundred and fifty feet of clear fire in every direction.

The fire from the tree line was quite heavy, along with rocket and mortars going off around us. The machine gun was white hot and it looked like the bullets were straightening out the barrel. I used my M-14 to relieve the team so they could exchange barrels. I was also relaying fire directions to my radio man who was in the process of calling in fire from artillery. That's when I was hit with shrapnel in my left knee. My radio man was excellent coordinating with Puff the Magic Dragon, Spooky, and artillery

at the same time. My squad members were laughing and cracking jokes and worked like a fine oiled machine. A grenade hit the pig pen and the pigs got out. That's when one of my men suffered a concussion. We took him to the doc in the basement.

Puff the Magic Dragon was a helicopter with mini guns that could cover a football field in a one second burst and put a round in every square foot. Spooky was a C130 aircraft with five mini guns and had twice the fire power as the helicopter. The enemy used green tracers and we used red tracer rounds.

When the mini-guns went off it looked like ray guns. One of the enemies was shooting three or four rounds at the gun ship and then ducking into a bunker. This went on for three or four times until the gun ship fired two bursts one after the other. The enemy had come out one time too many.

We stayed in position all night because we had the superior position. We would have exposed ourselves to a larger force if we had moved. We had a one-hundred-and-fifty-foot

clear field of fire and none of us was killed. Why would we expose ourselves to enemy fire? I was there to protect my men and to kill anyone that threatened them. I was the squad leader that the officers chose to go into the field with, because I used proper squad formations and I got my men home safe. The only officer that stupidly exposed Marines to enemy fire just happened to be my Platoon leader. I didn't lose any men in my squad until he was in charge. For this ambush which I led, I received a Bronze Star with a V device for Valor. I also received my second Purple Heart. I was taken out of the Infantry unit and assigned to The Battalion rear as the Police Sergeant. This action was unusual because they made up this position just for me. I was not used to being protected; I was used to being the protector. It was now my job to take the people charged with extra duty to go into the villages and find new Banana plants in order to line the Battalion C.P. walk way. I assigned a Quonset Hutt; I bought a refrigerator from which I could sell cold, sodas.

The President of the United States takes pleasure in presenting the
BRONZE STAR MEDAL to

LANCE CORPORAL DANIEL E. MC COY

UNITED STATES MARINE CORPS

for service as set forth in the following

CITATION:

"For heroic achievement in connection with combat operations against the enemy in the Republic of Vietnam while serving as a Squad leader with Company K, Third Battalion, First Marines, First Marine Division. On the night of 14 October 1969, Lance Corporal McCoy's squad had established an ambush in Quang Nam Province. When approximately twenty-five enemy soldiers came within range, Lance Corporal McCoy skillfully directed the fire of his men, inflicting several casualties upon the hostile force. When the enemy returned fire on the Marines with small arms, rocket-propelled grenades, and mortars, Lance Corporal McCoy and five of his squad members were wounded. Subsequently the numerically superior hostile force attempted to surround the Marines, however, Lance Corporal McCoy quickly positioned his machine gun team and his grenadier where they could effectively suppress the enemy fire. Despite his painful wound, he valiantly directed the efforts of his men throughout the night, as the hostile soldiers repeatedly probed the Marine position and were repulsed by the squad each time. As a result of his inspiring example and constant encouragement, his men successfully defended their position until morning, when the enemy withdrew. Lance Corporal McCoy's courage, aggressive leadership and unwavering devotion to duty in the face of great personal danger were in keeping with the highest traditions of the Marine Corps and of the United States Naval Service."

The Combat Distinguishing Device is authorized.

FOR THE PRESIDENT,

H. W. Buse jr

H. W. BUSE, JR.
LIEUTENANT GENERAL, U. S. MARINE CORPS
COMMANDING GENERAL, FLEET MARINE FORCE, PACIFIC

Dear dad,

I don't know if I have told you but I have been written up for the Bronze Star because I was in command of what was considered a perfect ambush.

We killed 5 VC, but only found two bodies and wounded about 7 VC. My squad had no wounded but had 1 person with a concussion. We found 1 AK 47.

Brad Miles was also written up for the Bronze Star; he was my radio operator. We were both written up for Meritorious Combat promotions for Corporal.

Well, so much for the Viet Nam Stories.

How is everyone at home? Tell Linda and Patty to write. I know I wrote them last and haven't received a reply. They better quit bugging me about writing if they won't themselves.

Well, got to go now.

Love,
Danny

SIXTY-ONE

The Chaplain went to the Armed Forces Exchange and convinced them to send the close to expire beer to our Battalion. The beer arrived on two low boy flatbed trucks. The Battalion Commander decided it was too much beer to hand out at once, so it was stored in my Quonset Hutt. My home became a favorite hangout for some senior Non-Commissioned Officers. It is amazing how popular you get when you have free beer to hand out.

I asked for a move to a Mortar team on another hill. This new base camp needed a clear field of fire so the Captain had them dump Agent Orange on and around our base camp.

This time I got a rash all over my body. I went to the Corpsman and he put the acid they used for athletes' foot all over my body. I was on fire. I jumped up and ran naked around the platoon base. I'm sure it was quite funny.

One day a sniper fired into the platoon base. The gunnery sergeant grabbed a rifle and ran into the village. He found the sniper and tried to shoot him but there was no clip in the rifle. He butted the sniper in the head with the empty rifle and ran back to the platoon base crying "who's the dumbass that has an unloaded rifle in a combat zone". I just got in a gunfight with a club. That is what you call a rifle without it being loaded. In a combat zone anything that delays you from firing a rifle is insanity, that includes trigger key locks and gun safes. I believe you should teach your children all about firearms and if you are too lazy to gun proof your children, you should learn how to use a baseball bat and keep a shovel next to the door. Do not teach children that guns are toys, unless you have gun proofed your children.

Thirty days to go and I was transferred to Headquarters Platoon. I had all my personal stuff ready to go, when I got a Dear John letter from my girl. I was pissed off, but what can you do. I volunteered to go on ambushes so I could take it out on my enemy, but that didn't work. On top of that, they also stole my hi-fi equipment at the Head quarter supply and they didn't send the sound equipment home to me. I had a Teac twenty ten real to real recorder, a set of big Pioneer speakers and Amplifier with top of the line turn table. People are never what they seem. I really miss my audio equipment.

I was told that some girls have a lot of military boyfriends in hope of receiving their death benefit. Twenty five thousand dollars is a lot of money in 1970. How was I to know that a seventeen year old girl was a Prostitute? I had a portrait and some silk pillows I had ordered custom made. When I got home I went to her house. When her parents answered the door, they told me I couldn't see her, and that she didn't want to see me. I told them I didn't want to see her. I just didn't want to keep the shit I

had made for her. I gave the items to them and walked away.

Dear mom,

I am sending $115 for Christmas presents and I would like you to give Patty $20 dollars to buy Gloria something and tell me what she buys her.

How is everything at home now? I am now a police sergeant in the H&S Co. Now it's a pretty good job and I hope I can do a good job at it. I have so far but it has it's complications as any job does. I am out of the bush and that is a good thing in itself as I can't gripe any about any amount I have to do. As a corporal I am not required to work on the working parties I am in charge of, but I do anyway.

Well, I am going to sign off now.

Love Always,
Danny

Dear dad,

How is everything at home? I hope the fishing and hunting is good. How was the deer hunting season this year? The crappie should be biting now. Have you had any luck lately?

How is the racial trouble in Vegas now, it is better or worse and are the girls having any trouble with the Niggers? I get along real well with the Negroes here but I'm a little too big for them to bully.

Did you see the pictures I sent Linda? I guess I look a little rough but that's to be expected I guess. Dad, I want to impose on you a little, would you send me a quart of Rum light? I don't want it to get drunk on but I do like to drink once in a while and it would probably last for a month. I don't like to go to the NCO club and I usually end up sitting with a bunch of friends and get drunk. If you do sent it put it in a bigger box with cans

of potted meat and smoked oysters and pickled pig's feet. I'll bet I sound like a leech. I can't get any of that over here.

Dad, really how is Linda getting along, does she still the infection? Is there a problem in getting it cleared up? I've heard different stories and I want the truth and if it gets bad I want you to send for me through the Red Cross.

I might be home by the time Patty graduates, also by the time Gloria graduates. I might get a 10 day cut and will probably be home by the 27th of May if I don't it will still be 2nd of June and it might take a while to get out of Okinawa anyway the time is getting short and I won't be sad to leave Viet Nam.

Give everybody my love. God bless you all and I send my prayers.

Your Son,
Love
Danny

Dear mom,

A burgundy turtleneck sweater would go good with the green suit or else a yellow turtleneck with a great big peace chain. Tell him to grow a mustache and sideburns and long hair, then we can call him daddy cool.

How is Wally Walruses coming along? When came for Christmas did he hit dad with his peace beads and swing at him with his sign yelling police brutality.

What's wrong with my Uncles? Is there some king of disease going around? None of them seem to be satisfied with being normal.

Did Uncle Pat show you all the new dances and speak the latest jive or did he just sit down and pucker up? I think I'm disgusted.

All you needed to fix the house up was Uncle Tom. Then you could have had everything California has; Hippies

and Queers and also probably a little police brutality when Uncle Tom started swinging his purse and Uncle Pat sat down to meditate. I don't know how dad put up with it.

I'm glad to hear anyway that everyone enjoyed Christmas.

That's great that Linda is getting married. I'm so happy for her. I'm glad to hear she is better.

The cookies were only half mashed and were quite good.

Well, got to go to sleep now.

Love,
Danny

Dear mom and dad,

Only 12 days left and they will probably be the longest I've spent since I've been in the Corps. I'm not ashamed to admit it I'm homesick, it's been five months since I spent any time with you all and I'm feeling pretty rough. I'm sick of all the shit that goes on here all the harassment.

It's all so senseless now. I can understand it when I was in boot camp and ITR and but it's just not sensible here even though I am in Mortar school. The more I train the more I hate the USMC. It might get better. The training is real good but it's the people in the Corp and the Corp isn't what it's supposed to be. Instructors always doing things they aren't supposed to do and some of them could get busted for it if some of us wanted to ruin our careers to get slack. I can take it for 12 more days but I don't know if it comes to

more than that, I'm pretty well fed up with everything.

I hope Kevin isn't getting worse. I was going to call today but I couldn't get off this area. Sorry I'm so harsh in my writing but that's the way I feel about it and I know it's a pretty dangerous way of thinking; it's pretty lousy to keep us here over Christmas for the first time in 16 years.

The recruiter said I would be home in 14 weeks, that's a laugh; it's almost been twice that long. I spent 9 weeks in boot camp, 7 to 6 weeks in ITR, and 3 weeks, it's all a big farce, all you hear about the Marines is the good part and even that's not so great, there aren't many people that want to join it.

18 weeks is quite a lot of time for a MNCRD an to be away from everyone he knows or cares anything without a break and I'm far from the only one who feels that way even some of instructors can't see keeping us here over Christmas. They really didn't gain anything by keeping us and they lowered our morale quite a bit.

I'll buy everyone a Christmas present when I came home quite a bit late I know, but it will still be in good faith.

Love All,

CHAPTER

SIXTY-TWO

My father wanted me to wear my uniform to Church. The first person I was introduced to was a local judge, who politely informed me that if I put my hands on anybody, he would throw the book at me and throw me in prison. Because of the disrespectful attitude of that Judge I did not get the message that he was trying to put across, I now realize that he was trying to tell me that no one has the right to put their hands on anyone in anger. This part of the law crosses all religions, races and ethnic groups. This must be taught to all religions, races and ethnic groups or it will be used to put them in prison. People who understand

this fundamental law can use it as a weapon to imprison any and all ethnic groups, no one has the right to act out in anger if it involves on laying their hands on anybody.

Then I went to a youth bible study. A very popular entertainer at that time named Pat was telling the class and informed me that God was not with us in Viet-Nam. I informed him that God may not be in him, but God was with me in Viet-Nam. I got up and walked out of the class. I had two grenades explode five feet behind me. I was in the kill radius of those two grenades. You explain how I'm still alive. I believe God was with me.

My best friend was called Brad Pie. We came home from Vietnam together. We were obviously not hippies. We bought wigs and hippie jeans to go out, but they thought we were hit men under cover, so that didn't work so very well. We wound up in the Las Vegas casinos. We lost about 3,000 dollars apiece. We then started bowling for the rest of our leave. We got pretty good because we bowled all day.

Dear mom & dad,

I'm having a bible sent home and as soon as you get it you have to write me back immediately because that's when I start paying for it. Whatever you do don't let anything happen to that bible. In the United States it's worth about $150 or more dollars. I'm paying $45 for it. The lettering on it is 24 karat gold.

Now that I've wrote my business transaction. How is everything at home? I'm doing fine. Last night we got mortared but nobody was hurt.

Brad and I are in the same pit. Same squad. How's that hurt? Don't look like we'll ever be separated.

We go out in the field in three or four days, so pray for me.

I don't know why but even over here I have a sense of security that I guess I shouldn't have, but I trust in God more

every day and I feel he will bring me through this. Well, I will sign off now.

> *Love Always,*
> *Danny*

CHAPTER

SIXTY-THREE

My sisters Linda and Patty both graduated from Western High School in Las Vegas. Linda was working as a secretary for the Retail Clerks Union and was engaged. Linda was self-supporting and independent, had her own apartment and did not move with the family when they moved to Idaho.

My father decided he would prefer to live life less complicated. They had visited his brother Bob in Bonners Ferry, Idaho the previous summer and decided to move there if at all possible.

They sold the house and loaded up to leave for God's country, Bonners Ferry, Idaho. Every

place we didn't live was God's country. Can you spell Post Traumatic Stress Disorder?

My sister Becky did not want to go to Idaho so she hid out with her friends so she couldn't be forced to go. No one wants to be tagged with the sign that says I Da Ho. The people that had bought the house were there waiting to move into the house, so they had to leave Becky behind. Uncle Pat was coming with us to help with the move and Sister Patty was going to Bonners Ferry also. They left air fare with my sister Linda so she could put Becky on a plane as soon as she showed up. My mother was driving the car with the camp trailer behind and was crying while trying to drive as they left Las Vegas. All she could do was to pray to God to keep Becky safe. In 1970 I was in the Marine Corp and did not take part in the move.

CHAPTER

SIXTY-FOUR

Washington D.C. was not what I expected. I had never experienced a town that was 95% of people with dark pigment skin. The drug problem was horrendous. The number two drug outlet was a pharmacy across the street from the front gate of Eighth and I South East, which is the location of the Marine Corps Barracks. I was stationed there. They told us there were on average six deaths a day and the bodies were lined up by the Garbage collectors for the police dept. to locate and the coroners Dept. to pick up and take to the hospital morgue for autopsy. The police dept. recruited the Honor Guard heavily. They also told us the likely hood of

getting mugged was very high. They told us not to go out alone.

One of our Marines thought that it was a lie. He went out by himself, because "those were his people". He came back in an hour with bloody knuckles and informed us that they were not his people and that we should go out in groups. In that area they are equal opportunity muggers. They don't care what color you are, they are going to mug you anyway. One of the guys said that the only program he watched on TV was Miami Vice because it was the only reality program on TV to watch.

A young marine from South Carolina was standing guard at the front gate of the oldest post of the Marine Corps. A totally smashed woman was trying to convince him to have sex through the gate. She was stripping and grinding her hips on the gate. I can understand the fantasy, but the young sergeant was a little bit confused as to how to handle the situation. He called back to the guard shack, which was the right thing to do, but we had to mess with him just a little bit. We asked him how old

he was. We asked if he was still a virgin. Was she asking for compensation? We went out and politely asked her to leave and thank you for the show. We had fun that way. He thought it was pretty funny too.

I got to the Home of the Presidential Honor Guard. 8th & I St. S.E. in June of 1970. Going from combat to Dress Blues is an interesting ordeal. The discipline is the same, the environment and objectives change. The perfectly fitted dress blues. My legs were too large for my waist size, so they had to give me 36 size trousers and cut the waist to 32. My chest was 48 so my coat had to be special ordered. All of my medals had to be anodized so they wouldn't tarnish. I received Corfram shoes, but I found out I was allergic to the shoes and the black socks. I could put cotton socks under the black nylon socks, but I had to use leather shoes that I had to spit shine all of the time. We used Mop and Glow with a cotton swab to protect our spit shine.

All of the Marines at the barracks were issued an M-1 Garand from surplus and we had to

put a show finish on our rifle. That entailed scraping the old oil and varnish off of the old stock with broken glass. Then we started the process of rubbing true oil on the cleaned stock. The more coats of true oil you rubbed in, the more glass like the coating became.

When we were in combat, it was just as important to make sure everything was black. Now the concentration was Shined brass and no black smudges on the white gloves and belts. No shined equipment in combat and no dull finishes state side.

CHAPTER

SIXTY-FIVE

I would occasionally do security work. We went to Puerto Rico and I was able to see a friend of mine. He introduced me to his family. The homes in Puerto Rico are wonderful. You can tell how big the family is by the number of bedrooms built around an outside kitchen and patio.

One night I was out on the street when this pretty woman walked up to me and said there is room for you in here. I looked down and she was very pregnant. I said "No thank you". She said, "How about a sixty eight"? I said "what is a sixty eight"? She said, "I do you and you owe me one". We had a good laugh.

It was unfortunate, Two weeks after my visit Joe was riding his motorcycle and ran off the road into a three strand fence and was killed instantly. What a waste of a good man. It is very hard to understand when a Marine goes through combat in a war and then senselessly dies shortly after returning home.

CHAPTER

★

SIXTY-SIX

In the U.S.M.C., You are not supposed to salute an officer when under an overhang. A young second lieutenant decided to chew the Sergeant Major of the post of the Marine Corps up one side and down the other, because the Sergeant Major had not saluted him under an overhang. The Sergeant Major took it calmly, then for some reason the young Lieutenant received orders to Yuma, Arizona. We called it, "How to go from the Post of the Marine Corps, to the anus of the Marine Corps". The Sergeant Major of the post of the Marine Corps is second only to the Sergeant Major of the Marine Corps. He was also the golf partner of the Commandant of the Marine Corps.

SIXTY-SEVEN

One of the most important things you learn in the Corps is the need for setting priorities. God, family, country and corps, this has been drummed into my head all of my life. You have got to have priorities in order to have success in life. You also need friends. Friends require a certain amount of trust. I am a big man and I have very little trust. I have plenty of opponents who want to gain my trust. People who try to destroy what they cannot control so I trust people to hide behind their position of illusive or imagined authority when they try to do you damage. It is not safe to attack me in person. I know that I am a well-developed

killing machine. I just choose to love the creator, love learning and choose to be good. Learning and choose to do good all of my days. This is my choice. It is not a commandment and I believe that God respects my freedom of will. I also believe that when you attack a man of God without provocation you are subject to the destruction of the flesh in order to preserve the soul, which is also part of our legal system.

The thief comes but for to kill, steal and destroy. All of these things are illegal under the law resulting in the destruction of the flesh for the preservation of the soul.

The Sergeant Major chose to make me a part of the command section so that I only answered to him and the other two colonels in the command section. I was made the driver. When I wasn't driving I seemed to be a popular bar tender for private parties. That was quite an eye opener to me. I saw things a young cowboy should not have to witness.

I became bored and disillusioned by the routine and dysfunction of Washington D.C. so I re-enlisted to become a recruiter.

CHAPTER

SIXTY-EIGHT

I was surprised to find myself assigned to the people rebuilding the Steam Boilers at the post of the Marine Corps. I loved it, two months of doing something simple. We had to saw all of the asbestos boards so they could bend all of the boards around the boilers. We then wrapped the boiler in asbestos cloth and we painted the whole boiler in asbestos paint. It was assumed to be inert, nontoxic rocks. I mean, how can rock dust hurt you? We didn't wear masks. Ignorance is bliss.

Recruiters' school was possibly the school I used the most. I was used to fighting and giving

orders but public speaking was as scary as it gets for me. I really was quite bashful.

Security starts with the recruitment program. The applications are designed to weed out criminals and malcontents. You can apply for mercy through the waiver system. I must say the inspection of your life gets intent the more trouble you have experienced or accidents you have had. Circumstances do determine the choices made to overlook malcontent or accidents related to youth full exuberance. The marine corps is looking for warriors.

The Marine Corps is a huge business and is always looking for qualified applicants. Basic training takes care of the ninety day trial period and is designed to weed out those applicants not likely to be able to survive in the military.

CHAPTER

SIXTY-NINE

Arecruiter is a very finely trained salesman. They must have a basic understanding of the various jobs in the military and the basic requirements, physical and intellectual, required for entry level into the different jobs in the military. The entry level tests are based on a sixth-grade reading level test. I once tested 21 High School Graduates and only three passed the test.

Public speaking is interesting. To go from bashful to speaking to entire school audiences is to realize most people do want to hear what you are talking about. It is also important to their future. The military is one of the largest

employers in the world. It is amazing how the armed serviced vocational aptitude battery {ASVAB} can be used by all branches of the service. It works if some dumb shit officer can follow the design and stick to the program. Many officers believe they are smarter than the proven track. That is when screw ups happen. Once they learn that the system is smarter than they are they are usually promoted to their highest level of incompetence. Getting officers out of the way is one of the ways Sergeants' get things done. Officers are a simple redundancy looking for a place to mean something. Make no mistake, there are many wonderful men wearing Officers uniforms, I just didn't have the luxury of serving under them.

MY NEED

In the darkness of my thoughts
I condemn only those without fault.
I do not like them,
Nor do I wish to be around them.
I must help those I am with
Or I cannot find contentment.
For I am a hypocrite.
Unless I can find fault,
I cannot find happiness.

By Daniel E. McCoy

WAR SONG

Closing an
Surrounding
Deep within
Exploding
Body tense
Convulsing
Slipping-by
Creeping
Down my side
Battle
Human flesh
Metal
Patience thin
Breath
Another man
Death
With medals
Success
With guilt
I rest
In peace

By Daniel E. McCoy

LOVE THE CREATOR
LOVE THE STUDY OF CREATION
CHOOSE TO DO GOOD
ALL THE DAYS OF YOUR LIFE
AS TAUGHT BY THE RABI, JESUS CHRIST
MESSIAH
MY BROTHER

You have the right to choose not become angry
You can stop people from manipulating your life
This is the key to success in America
Keep your hands off other People
There is no situation where you have the right to
put your hands on another person in anger.

By Daniel E. McCoy

Anyone that tells you that you have the right to
your anger either wants something you've got or
wants to put you in jail.

Education:

Bayou Elementary School, Gulfport, Mississippi

Western High School, Las Vegas, Nevada

Fort Steilacoom Community College, Fort Steilacoom, Washington

Associates and Technology Degrees:

University of Main, Orono, Maine: Bachelor of University

Studies

The Dahan Institute of Massage Therapy, Las Vegas, Nevada

USMC 1968 - 1975

www.ingramcontent.com/pod-product-compliance
Lightning Source LLC
Chambersburg PA
CBHW070916120626
46546CB00001B/287